D0531527

NM 9/17

Please return/renew this item by the last date shown on this label, or on your self-service receipt.

To renew this item, visit **www.librarieswest.org.uk** or contact your library.

Your Borrower number and PIN are required.

Libraries**West**

4 1 0054 127 7

Run, Ride, Sink or Swim

A year in the exhilarating and
addictive world
of women's triathlon

LUCY FRY

FABER & FABER

First published in 2015
by Faber & Faber Limited
Bloomsbury House
74–77 Great Russell Street
London WC1B 3DA

Typeset by Faber & Faber Limited
Printed and bound by CPI Group (UK) Ltd, Croydon, CRO 4YY

A CIP record for this book
is available from the British Library

ISBN 978–0–571–31314–3

FSC
www.fsc.org
MIX
Paper from
responsible sources
FSC® C101712

2 4 6 8 10 9 7 5 3 1

To all those women who want to tri
but think they can't – this book is for you
because you can

Prologue

A large wave slaps me on the cheek and I swallow another mouthful of salty water. We have been going for thirty minutes. Open water swimming, they call it, but I'd say it was more like *relentless semi-drowning*. I'm grumbling silently to myself that even when I take a breather I have to wriggle my legs and arms around to stay afloat. There are no lane barriers or poolside pauses here, just a wide stretch of ocean between the Grenadine Islands of Palm and Union. Today's task is to cross it. I'm here in the Caribbean to write about what it's like to take swimming lessons from the Olympic gold medallist Rebecca Adlington and her fiancé, Harry Needs, who is also a competitive swimmer in his own right. I've had two lessons in the resort pool but this is the big challenge: 1.8 kilometres of open water. That's just under a nautical mile, with a mild but noticeable current to boot.

Is this really in my job description? A freelance writer does all sorts of things in the name of work, even leaving their spouse in London for a week to battle a fear of the open sea. As for whether it might be in keeping with my nature, the answer is yes and no. Yes to challenging myself; to using my body in pursuit of new experiences. No to swim caps, goggles and doing things as a team.

'Enjoying it?' shouts the trip's organiser, Karen, who's sensibly decided to remain on the boat to 'keep watch' over the five bikini-clad journalists involved.

'Oh yeah!' I yell across the increasingly powerful waves, trying to sound as flippant as possible. 'Totally loving it.'

Is it obvious that I'm lying? I've always maintained that I vehemently dislike swimming – almost certainly because I'm convinced that I'm not naturally any good at it. But five minutes ago, for about eight strokes, I stopped thinking how much I'd rather be lying in a hammock and felt a sense of . . . pleasure. I moved through the water freely, without struggling for breath or thinking about the placement of my arms or the unsophisticated splash created by my legs. For at least ten seconds, I was actually present, in the moment and – shock horror – enjoying myself.

And then that wave arrived.

Now I feel, yet again, like a weighted lump discolouring the perfect blue water. What's the appeal of open water swimming, I wonder? Particularly back in the UK, where, I'm told, you have to pee in your wetsuit to keep warm. Apparently there are techniques that can be learned, practised and perfected. If you tilt your head slightly up and further to one side when taking a breath (further than would be advisable for efficient freestyle swimming in a pool), for example, you can take a look around and search for landmarks, establishing whether you're zig-zagging all over or actually going in the right direction. If you keep your elbow high, you can ideally reach over the waves and, according to Harry, who loves open water swimming, 'grab on to the water'. He also tells me which kick 'beat' I'm using. Apparently they come in twos, fours and sixes, though two is best for preserving energy on longer swims. But right now the only beat I hear is my heart. With a mouth like a salt-cellar and the constant sense that a jellyfish might be about to nibble my feet, I keep forgetting details of Harry's pep talks on technique. The only thing I remember throughout the entire swim, in fact, is that I am wearing a swimming cap lent to me by Becky Adlington herself. Yes! There may be a stray blonde Olympian hair atop my scalp! Will it make me faster? Make me look less like I'm drowning, perhaps?

At last I approach the shore, paddling the final fifty metres like a shipwrecked dog. I am greeted by the faster two members of our party (the bastards are virtually dry already) and, much to my surprise, followed by Becky, who I appear to have 'beaten' to the finish. Though she is one of the greatest female freestyle swimmers Great Britain has ever had, winning two gold medals at the Beijing 2008 Olympics and two bronze medals at London 2012, she admitted yesterday that she hates the sea. Harry says he's only ever seen her go knee-deep in it during the two and a half years they've been dating. But today, halfway across our gauntlet and to everyone's (including her own) amazement, she threw away years of terror and jumped in to help round up a few struggling swimmers who'd become separated from the group. Not me, I hasten to add; I had Becky Adlington's swim cap so didn't need her actual help.

There's an outpouring of congratulations when she steps out of the water.

'Becky, wow! You went in the sea! You swam open water!' Harry says.

'Yay,' I mumble, not even trying to hide my sarcasm as

I'm handed a can of Coke – supposedly the ideal antidote to the nauseating pollution and salt in the water we've swallowed.

If she wasn't one of the nicest women I've ever met, I'd be positively miffed that Becky is *still* getting all the attention. What's more, when I wasn't guzzling my Coke with slightly pathetic enthusiasm, I'd be thinking how she must only have *half* the pollution in her body that we have in ours, considering she only travelled *half* the distance. But I'm suddenly strangely incapable of doing much other than smiling.

My body is being flooded with endorphins. But it's more than just a chemical reaction – I'm feeling proud, and excited – this is emotional too. Because the entire distance that I'm looking out at . . . I actually *swam* that. All. By. Myself.

What else could my body do, I wonder? I thought I knew my limitations, but now I'm forced to question them. What else might I achieve, if I threw away my fears and dived right in?

1

Sometimes you don't really know when something – an idea, obsession or characteristic – started to grow until, fully immersed in it, you look back and see the roots trailing behind you. So it is with triathlon and me. I think perhaps it begins when I am very young – five or six years old – and first display the traits of a perfectionist, training for and worrying about school sports day as if it were an Olympic qualifier. Maybe it comes later, in my twenties with my foray into distance running, which leads in turn to a series of injuries that mean I quickly learn the benefits of cross-training. Or perhaps it is London 2012, watching the television screen in awe as the GB triathletes Alistair and Jonathan Brownlee take gold and bronze medals and Helen Jenkins continues an uphill struggle against injury to come in fifth in the women's race.

How does it feel to run straight off a bike? I wonder as I watch. And what about cycling straight after swimming? Doesn't that feel weird, when you're still wet? That swim start looks aggressive. So does the rest of the race, in fact. And as for the transitions where they move from swim to cycle, and cycle to run? Those seem to involve the kind of speedy costume changes that would make a catwalk model nervous.

A year passes and – here is where it most obviously begins – it is August, another summer drawing to a close. I am thirty-one years old and have just spent nearly ninety minutes fighting off Caribbean waves and developing some rather impressive tan lines on my back during my first organised open water swim. I am re-emerging onto dry land when I hear a local talking to another member of our group.

'If you thought that swim was hard you should come back here in three months' time. The nearby island of St Lucia is holding its first triathlon.'

Immediately, my interest is piqued. Over recent years I've noticed triathlon becoming increasingly popular with friends and acquaintances. Long gone are the days when this three-legged sport was the preserve of professional athletes and serious amateurs. I know busy women with demanding jobs and active social lives – some with children and partners too – who used to relish their weekend downtime and wouldn't have been seen dead in the Lycra onesie also known as a trisuit. Those same women now choose to rise at dawn on summer Sundays to don unflattering all-in-one waterproof skins and swim–bike–run their way to glory.

I quite enjoy running but, despite those few positive moments in the Caribbean, I suspect I still hate swimming. When it comes to cycling, I've had the occasional enjoyable ride but on the whole the bike and I have never really gelled. The idea of putting all three together? It's partly laziness (three sports in one – I can't be arsed) and partly fear (three sports in one = three lots of potential failure) but really, I can't see much appeal.

Yet most people know me as a sporty person, the kind of woman who would or should, most likely, be obsessed with triathlon. It's not just the physical rewards of exercise that I love – it's also the mental ones. During the nearly fifteen years since I first bought a gym membership, taking exercise has helped me to combat recurring bouts of anxiety and depression more successfully than any pharmaceutical drug. It's a very subjective thing, of course, but for me, when nerves are frayed and the familiar bugle call of *can't* or *won't* or *just too shit* chimes in my head, I've learned over the years that I must *do*, rather than *think*, wherever possible. It's never quite as bad when you return. So long as you move, there will be a minute, or a few seconds, when all you're thinking about is co-ordinating your joints, or the ache in your muscles. Crank up the volume on any workout and it'll leave you with a slight numbness for a couple of hours afterwards: relief for the anxious, respite for the heartbroken and Mecca for the depressed.

I'm not sure how much longer I can deal with being ritually exposed as a fitness junkie who hasn't tri-ed. There must be something magical here, after all, otherwise why is the world going nuts for a sport that first arrived on British shores in 1983 and whose first Olympic appearance was just thirteen years ago? Hell, even my mother, who never learned to ride a bike, now knows the component parts of triathlon, since her neighbour started collecting sponsorship to enter one in September.

Enough's enough. I think back to that moment on the beach immediately after stepping onto the shore and that mention of triathlon. Thousands of miles from home and yet the sport continues to suggest itself, taunting me into action. I can't sit on the sidelines any longer, particularly not now I know I'm capable of open water swimming, however badly, the distance required of me in a standard tri. It's time I did my bit for gender equality anyway; while female participation in the average triathlon has undoubtedly risen incrementally over recent years, most start lines remain just twenty-five per cent female. I quite fancy joining the other ladies and giving those MAMILS (middle-aged men in Lycra) a swim, bike and run for their money.

Most importantly, perhaps it's time I let go, once and for all, of the failure complex I've been living with. Throughout my twenties and teens, and a good few years before that, I never felt satisfied. Every achievement was quickly subsumed by the next goal; every accomplishment eclipsed by the remaining shortfalls. Moving into my thirties, I've begun to see the useless nature of such an approach. I want to learn to accept the previously unacceptable, that is to say, myself. This process has already begun, as I've become a little more moderate and less idealistic about both relationships and work. When it comes to sport and training, however, I still feel a constant pressure to surpass my own expectations – forever disappointed with my foibles and inevitable ageing. Will I ever change? I still want to set targets – to try and blast through limits and challenge myself – but can I do so whilst accepting that I'm imperfect and won't always succeed?

Triathlon, so multifaceted and so intense, might prove the acid test.

It is that August, on the plane back to London from Palm Island, that I first begin to mull it over. I briefly consider setting a date for my first triathlon in April or May the next year but that seems a long way off. My curiosity is aroused now, and it won't just sit around waiting for the entire winter.

The idea begins to fizz. Spend a year doing triathlon: now that's a plan of action. But how to shape that year? This sport has a calendar all of its own, revolving mostly around 'the season' and 'the off season'. The two parts are very distinct: 'the season' is the time of year when the skies are less likely to darken and the skin less likely to shiver, i.e. May to September. During this time the game is on; it's a period of intense focus, all about training for races and the races themselves. 'The off season' refers to any months that don't fall within that time, and it often involves building muscle, addressing injuries, eating more and generally dealing with parts of life – people, relationships, careers, other sports or hobbies – that are sidelined during the season.

I'll need to experience gametime as well as downtime if I'm to really get a sense of a triathlete's life. Somewhere over the Atlantic a more structured plan starts forming: I'll live through two main 'seasons', endless training and a handful of races – five sounds rigorous but feasible. I'll take advantage of the varying distance options in triathlon, starting small with a couple of sprint distance events, slowly building my body and brain up to a longer grand finale. I could begin training in earnest this autumn and then do my first event next May when the season starts in the UK. But that would mean clustering all the races within just a few months. This raises the chance of injury or burnout. Also, lovely as it sounds to officially begin my year in triathlon during the off season, it seems a little pointless if there hasn't yet been any *on*.

Then I remember the St Lucia Triathlon. It's in late November – not around the corner but not too far away either. It being an inaugural event, I'm guessing there will be a small field of participants, a party atmosphere and plenty of beginners. Once that's done, I'll crank things up a little.

By the time my plane lands in London, I have a clearer idea of what's required. One year. Five triathlons. What could possibly go wrong?

2

Back in the UK, there are excuses. First I am 'recovering' from the exertions of the island-to-island swim, then it's jet lag and after that I'm 'looking for the right pool'. Before I know it, it's been four weeks since (with the exception of taking a bath) I have dunked my body in water. Somehow that tangible sense of possibility that I'd felt back on Palm Island has become tarnished by the daily flow of urban life. Late-running trains, work deadlines, social engagements and the onset of colder weather: it all gets in the way and, while I've been out running and to the gym a few times since returning, I haven't yet practised my swimming. What's more, I haven't mentioned my idea of doing a year of triathlon to anyone, not even my wife, Bella, and now I'm wondering, really, is it worth the bother, after all?

One Sunday morning in mid September, mainly out of a desire to prove that it *was* all a silly pipe dream, that I can't possibly jet off to the Caribbean just for a triathlon, I finally head out for a swim. It's a luxurious ozone-treated pool linked to the plush central London gym where Bella is a member.

I drop into the water reluctantly. Using Bella's one-and-only guest pass for this establishment helps to guilt-trip me into staying longer. At least half an hour. Minimum.

I hold my breath and push off the wall with determined legs. Twenty minutes pass surprisingly easily. Has my technique improved a fraction? Becky Adlington's wise words cling to me as I do some of the drills she suggested: 'the catch', where you wait for one hand to arrive next to the other out in front before you take your next stroke, and 'the finger drag', which involves a rather camp trailing of the nails against the water as each arm extends above your head. But one thing hasn't changed: I splutter and gasp air in (think: cat with furballs) at the end of every length. How will I ever manage a sprint triathlon swim – 750 metres – or an Olympic – 1500 metres – without stopping?

Maybe I need a longer pool, I think, one where I have to stop fewer than thirty times before hitting the 750-metre mark. The following weekend, still mute about my half-arsed intentions to head out to St Lucia for the inaugural triathlon in seven weeks' time, I visit the Tooting Bec Lido. It's the UK's largest open-air freshwater swimming pool and, as luck would have it, a ten-minute walk from where I live. But in the six months that have passed since Bella and I moved into our new home – and, more revealingly, in the thirty-one years that I've lived in the surrounding area – I've never set foot inside.

Ninety-one metres long and thirty metres wide, it's more of a mini-lake than a pool. What's more, it's always unheated and on this cold autumnal day, the water temperature is approximately six degrees centigrade. I don't yet own a wetsuit, which isn't ideal. But there are plenty here without.

Hanging about nervously on the poolside, I strike up a conversation with cold water swimming old-timer Steven. 'Do triathletes come here to train?' I ask him, pointing to a couple of women in wetsuits doing front crawl.

'Yes, triathletes,' he sighs. 'It's a nightmare in the spring and summer when they come here. They have no idea about etiquette. I even had to chaperone one swimmer once just to keep the triathletes from clambering all over him. They think of swimming as a contact sport,' he adds.

The less said about my own sporting plans the better, I decide, and mumble my thanks to Steven before darting into an icy changing room to disrobe. Five minutes later and I'm costume-clad and ready to rumble. I hop from one leg to another, watching as others enter the water. Some go slowly and fearfully, just as you would when entering an excessively hot bath, whilst others splash in without so much as a second thought. Whichever way you do it, though, the body is in for a shock once it's submerged.

Here goes, I think. *And remember: this is the year of the triathlon. Your year of new experiences. A bit of cold water won't kill you.*

Grabbing the handles of the steps and turning around with my back towards the pool, I go down until the water is waist deep. So far so good. It's cold but not unbearable. But once my torso is in, everything changes; a rather debilitating breathlessness arrives. I cling to the edge of the pool and try to look relaxed, like this is something I've done every single day of my life.

Clearly, I'm not convincing; no more than thirty seconds pass before Steven comes to check that I'm OK. I try to answer him with a 'Yes, all fine,' but it appears my voice no longer works. All that comes out are short, sharp inhalations of breath. Tossing aside my pride, I manage, in fits and starts, to ask (gasp) for (gasp) a few (gasp) tips.

'Well, keep your mouth shut for a start,' says Steven.

I smirk; I don't think he means it as it sounds. And, in fact, he's absolutely right; I close my mouth and, miraculously, my lungs appear to open. I wonder if this is a good metaphor for my life (and training) in general; stop asking so many questions and your body will do what it needs to do.

'Now just take it really, really gently,' he says.

'OK,' I nod.

I'm not very good at doing things gently but in these temperatures it's hard to get anywhere fast. Small movements feel like huge ones, little breaths like big achievements. But, after a few lengths of breaststroke, a tickly heat begins to run through my blood as if matches are being lit against my skin. It's bizarrely pleasant and I feel a childish enthusiasm, grinning as I continue pulling myself through the water and not caring when small leaves lodge themselves down my cleavage.

Now, surely it's time to do some actual training, I think, and shove my head into the water with a view to beginning to practise the triathlete's favoured stroke: front crawl.

Snap! It's like a reflex action. My head bounces back up and out of the water. I try again but it's too cold.

'You should get out now,' says Steven.

'But I feel great!' I yell, with a twitch.

'And well you might,' he says. 'When you're in the water the blood goes to your core to keep you warm. But when you get out, it all goes to your extremities again, and you can get very, very cold. So the first few times you shouldn't do too much. You need to *acclimatise*.'

Acclimatise.

I've heard this word before whenever cold water swimming has been mentioned. And, just like 'gently', it's a word that brings out the sulky adolescent in me. I've only done four lengths! And breaststroke too! What planet is this man on? I'm here to train for triathlon! I'm not getting out yet – no way!

I push my head under the water. I want to do front crawl.

I manage about eight strokes in total before I absolutely have to stop.

The gap between body and mind has never felt vaster than it does right now. As if to add insult to respiratory injury, an elderly lady drifts past. She is slow but has near-faultless technique and looks as if she is barely making any effort at all. She is at least forty years older and three stone heavier than me.

She has clearly *acclimatised*. It is the final straw.

Time's up, I think, and slip as surreptitiously as possible out of the pool and into the ladies' changing room. It takes about five minutes (and is made only temporarily better by a long hot shower) but, sure enough, I soon find myself shivering uncontrollably. I'm not talking about a subtle, rather endearing chattering of the teeth, but about molars clacking against one another and hands that make large, uncontrollable movements. Being the convivial hub that it is, the lido club offers tea and coffee to shellshocked swimmers, but I can't even hold my cup without it spilling everywhere. I can only remember one other time in my life when I've felt this cold, and that was fifteen years ago and involved six hours of skiing in an unrelenting blizzard.

A few minutes later, though, things start to improve.

Warmth returns to my limbs and with it arrives a wondrous rush of wellbeing, joyfulness and – just as I've heard dedicated cold water swimmers promise – an almost tangible elation. The world is a brighter, tastier and generally more welcoming place than it was an hour ago, and on the return journey everything looks, smells and seems different. The outlines of the trees seem to be carved into the sky and a piquant winter dew finds its way into my nostrils. An overwhelming sense of possibility arrives in my heart. I may not have done much real exercise today but the way I feel is remarkably similar to how I felt five weeks ago after our big Caribbean swim. It's as if the shocking drop in body temperature has reset my internal systems, shaken me up and caused my resolve to re-emerge. One month down, eleven more to go, and now it's time to make the year of triathlon official and tell someone.

When I walk whistling back through the door, I find Bella at home, having returned earlier than scheduled from a weekend away.

'What on earth have you been doing?' she asks, looking at my wet hair.

'Swimming!' I say, still feeling as if I've taken something illegal.

In the five and a half years we've been together, Bella has never seen me smile while saying *swimming*. She's bound to know that something's up. Given my tendency towards excess, and having returned from Palm Island not much more than a month ago with mostly negative reflections on the experience of open water swimming, I'm understandably tentative about explaining my plans to her. Besides, we're quite different animals, my wife and I. It's not that Bella doesn't enjoy training, just that she isn't intense or addictive about it. When we met and fell quickly in love back in 2008, she was far from a regular gym-goer. We drank together, we smoked together and then, when we'd done enough drinking and smoking together, we went running together. Bella started to get the fitness bug and joined a gym. She went to classes and discovered a love of yoga. She ran a ten-kilometre race, and then a half marathon. She, like many other women I know, is healthier at thirty-three than she was at twenty-three. But, unlike me and plenty of other women I know, Bella is relaxed about the extra wobble that comes and goes around her stomach. She thinks nothing of eating dessert three nights in a row if she feels like it. She's never pushed herself to exercise when she's exhausted or stuffed up with cold, never continued to run when injured and advised by a physiotherapist to back off, and she's fairly scathing about the childish zeal with which fitness junkies (like me) discuss how many press-ups they can do before collapsing in a heap, demanding water, wine or both.

'I think I'm going to be doing some triathlons,' I start. 'There's one in the Caribbean. In November. Just a short one though. I might do that. And then, um, next year . . . I think I'll do one, or two more, ormaybethreeorfourorevenfive . . . maybe slightly longer . . . What do you think?'

I read her face for signs, trying to guess her thoughts: *Last*

year it was boxing. Recently it's been CrossFit. Now it's triath-
lon. Can't you just calm down a bit?

'But.' She tries to be tactful. 'Don't you still struggle, a bit, with swimming?'

I nod.

'And don't you kind of dislike cycling these days too?' she asks, just to be sure.

'Yes, but. Well, actually it's traffic I dislike more than riding a bike,' I sigh. 'But maybe it's time I faced that stuff anyway,' I say.

'That sounds like quite a lot of pressure to put on yourself.'

I agree. It could go wrong. But there is purpose beyond just the doing, I explain. Purpose in why and how too. This is part of a broader, ongoing pursuit – not just about figuring out what's so special about triathlon but also finding a balance between testing and accepting myself.

Bella is quiet for a while, taking it all in. I know she finds my energy and enthusiasm, broken up as it is by pockets of exhaustion and acute sadness, quite draining, and I'm fully aware that my spikes in mood make me tiring to live with. I can only hope that all this means Bella is already prepared for life as one half of a mixed marriage – where one is a triathlete and one isn't. I've heard about how triathlon can get between a couple. For the non-triathlete, all that re-enters the house on a Saturday afternoon after a fifty-mile cycle ride, for example, is a muddier, hungrier and achier version of the person he or she originally met and was attracted to. The triathlete cannot comprehend where the problem lies – they are fitter, happier, and look better naked, after all. The non-triathlete cannot understand where the increasingly dull obsession came from, and how it prospers. This is not the person he or she fell in love with! I don't want to risk that happening to us.

'Why don't we do one of these triathlons *together*?' I say to Bella. 'We could train *together*? Go for swims and runs and stuff?'

Bella looks at me like I'm a dog biting at her heels.

'I can't be bothered to learn front crawl,' she says. 'And I don't really ride a bike, remember?'

Ah. Yes. I remember, regretfully, the one and only time we went for a cycle ride together. We were on holiday in Menorca, soon after we'd got engaged. Renting bikes for an afternoon would be a fun way to explore the area, I persuaded her. But it wasn't. Bella wobbled slowly, on the verge of angry tears throughout, and I kept surging ahead by mistake, stopping occasionally to wait, yelling words of encouragement as she reappeared, furiously, through the humid dust.

Twenty-one days later and it's the morning of my second ever half marathon: a mass entry London event called Run to the Beat (because of the DJs and bands that play at every mile). It starts badly with a 3 a.m. nightmare that leaves me unable to return to sleep. By the time I leave the house at seven, I feel anxious, not just because I'm exhausted but also because of a problem in my left leg. Two days ago in the gym I pulled a weighted barbell off the ground and felt my hamstring twang. Straight afterwards it was stiff and irritated but now it's not too bad. Nonetheless, I worry: is this just a niggle, or something bigger – a full-blown injury?

This thought circulates for the entire tube journey to the event hub in Greenwich Park. Once the race starts, however, it disappears. The first few miles go by with relative ease as we charge off towards Blackheath.

Nearly an hour later and I am six and a half miles in. Another bead of sweat falls from my brow onto the ground below. This is how far it would be, I think to myself: the running portion of an Olympic distance triathlon would already be over by now. How my legs feel at this point in time, however, is almost certainly not how they might feel during a ten-kilometre run preceded by a 1500-metre swim and a (deep breath) forty-kilometre ride.

But still, it's a good sign?

A few minutes later something shifts. What had begun promisingly with a gradual release of energy, a quick warming of the muscles and around ten kilometres of steady running, is now beginning to tip over into fatigue. My body weakens and my legs become heavier with every step but the knowledge that there is more than six miles to go is the biggest issue of all. My thoughts begin to niggle. Up until this point I've managed to keep a lid on the inevitable, negative *I'm tired, what's the point* kind of thinking, to reassure myself that *this is good, just keep relaxed and breathe easy, you'll feel amazing when it's over*. But now I really am tired, more tired than I can remember being in a long time.

My sore hamstring, which has been virtually imperceptible thus far, begins to hurt again. It's a dull pain, more of an ache than a specific burning or pinpricking, but it's getting stronger with every passing step. It pushes me over the edge of despondence and into despair. Suddenly I'm not just having a tricky patch, I'm almost ready to give up.

How does that happen? At six and a half miles you're still 150 per cent invested in your race. By mile eight, you're almost ready to nip under the barrier and catch the next train home. Perhaps this is all part and parcel of my obsession with doing consistently well. I can't bear the thought of regressing in any way, or of having a bad race. I must always improve on my previous performance; I must be infallible, or else what? (I may as well give up.) It is, as I'm discovering, an oppressive and self-defeating attitude, though not an easy one to change.

I think it's more by luck than anything else that I continue; just at the point where I'm seriously considering stopping, the road narrows and I'm suddenly flanked by people on all sides. Together our feet smack percussively against the ground, a cacophony of rubber against concrete. I physically can't get out.

The road widens again. The black thoughts have become purple and I am no longer ready to give up. With an upright movement of the torso, I try to convince my body I'm not tired. And it works, just a tiny bit, just enough to keep me going, and going, and going, until, around the next bend, and then the next, there's the nine-mile marker and some music, some crowds . . .

I'm too close to the end to abandon this now. By the time I pass the ten-mile mark I am accustomed to the nagging soreness in my leg. The body's natural painkillers are kicking in and I know without a shadow of a doubt that I will finish whatever happens. That certainty, along with the boost from an energy gel I took ten minutes ago, brightens me further until, somehow, my body has revived itself and I pick up the pace in the final mile. But there's a steep hill on the horizon and it takes all my will and fury to get up it. The last three hundred metres are slow and dogged. I cross the line in one hour and forty-seven minutes, only a little disappointed that it is two minutes slower than my first half marathon last year.

I don't know it at the time, but it will be my last long run for seven months. The day after the half marathon the pain is bad and the day after that it is worse. A few weeks on, my left leg and hip area still ache portentously on a daily basis. Bending over with straight legs creates a strong tugging sensation all down my left side – not a muscle tightness that relaxes when stretched, but more like an elastic band, about to snap. During a very frustrating three or four weeks I see two sports professionals, a few times each, and spend a couple of hundred pounds on having myself manipulated, massaged and (the worst bit) needled. Neither of them knows for sure what I have done, nor can they offer much more definitive advice except *don't push it, no impact work* and *definitely no running*. Even if it was miraculously fixed tomorrow (which it won't be) there still wouldn't be much time to get any decent running training in before the triathlon in St Lucia. Thank goodness I've not been completely stupid and entered myself for the longest distance, but only for the 'sprint', which culminates in a five-kilometre run. Hopefully I can get round on sheer grit if nothing else. How much it will hurt is another matter.

3

By mid October I'm beginning to get a little anxious about the hugeness of what I've decided to do: to complete five swim–bike–run events – one in the Caribbean in just over five weeks and four next year – as part of this personal quest. I'm going to need some help if I'm to get through the next ten months without a) giving up, b) going mad, or c) getting divorced. I want a Dream Team of people around me, each with their own expertise, something unique to bring to the year-in-triathlon table. The most important of all is a Commitment Aide. In the past I have pursued new hobbies with a frantic fury until something untoward happens and, bang, just like that, I drop them completely. So I'll need someone to keep me on track for the one-year-five-triathlons experience. My triathlete friend Ren, perhaps? Head of operations for a small advisory firm in the banking industry, she's a thirty-seven-year-old, tough, blonde Irishwoman who has been living in west London for nearly a decade. We met a couple of months ago at a friendly CrossFit 'throwdown' where we competed against one another and five other women to see who was the fittest there. Let's just say that Ren didn't beat me at 'the sport of fitness' then but she has routinely done so since. What's more, after being teamed with Ren for a few strength-building, lung-busting workouts over the past few weeks, I can say with confidence that she hates whiners and doesn't mind shouting at me to *get a fucking move on*, all of which could be very useful traits in a Commitment Aide.

Secondly, I need a Tri Guide, someone with experience and expertise who can write training schedules for me and help me choose which events to do. Since I'm prone to catastrophising and losing perspective when small things get in the way of bigger objectives, he or she will need to be fairly zen, with a mature, intelligent world view. Last criterion: this can't be someone with whom I already have an emotional connection or I'll just whinge whenever I feel the need. A specialist triathlon coach, perhaps? Does such a person/thing exist? I'll add that to the Tri To-Do List: *Find myself a coach.*

Thirdly, I'll need to make some new triathlete friends, people of varying ages and abilities for whom triathlon is important. Total immersion = social immersion. My other friends will understand.

Fourthly and finally (for now), I'll need a Relationship Crisis Barometer. Knowing how overwhelming I find big projects and my need to talk about them, it's important to have a gauge that tells me when I'm becoming excessively self-involved. Ordinarily I get some major hints from the expression on my wife's face but, then again, usually these projects or obsessions don't last. This time, however, with a Commitment Aide on board, I won't be giving up and therefore I could get into trouble at home. I'll definitely need a contingency plan for Marital Rescue. Having been brought up a Catholic, there was a time in my life when a monk or two might have done the trick, but a questioning of faith combined, a few years later, with my current penchant for same-sex relations have put paid to that possibility. Instead I start asking around for advice, beginning with ex-triathlete friend Martin, who tells me merely that giving up triathlon was a proviso of his non-triathlete wife's agreeing to their engagement. Other people (those who don't know me very well, I might add) offer similarly unhelpful suggestions like *just don't talk about it at home* or *maybe just don't take it too seriously*. So I decide to look no further, rather paradoxically, than my wife herself. Surely she'll know better than anyone, after all, when she's beginning to find me unbearable?

'You'll need to tell me if I start becoming completely obsessed by triathlon,' I say one evening that October. (So far there aren't any signs but . . .) 'If I'm turning into a total bore, please tell me. Before it gets too late.'

Bella nods, a little too fervently.

Next I start sending messages to anyone I know who has an interest in triathlon or to whom I have spoken about the sport for more than twenty seconds. My friend Stewie, a yoga teacher at the studio where I practise, went to Lanzarote in the Canary Islands for a ten-day triathlon training camp earlier this year to get a taste of a new sport. Surely he met some keen female triathletes whilst he was there? I ask.

He soon replies: Yes, he did. Two women, a couple: Emily and Suzanne. He thinks they'd love to talk to me about it, and promises to make some introductions via email so we can arrange a meeting.

Next up is Ren: I call and ask if she'd be happy to help me, not just with some training here or there but also, more generally, to stay on track. Much to my terror, she laughs.

'Oh yes, all right then. I think I'm going to enjoy this.'

I'm pretty sure I can actually hear her rubbing her hands together.

No doubt about it now: the wheels are in motion. Now the time has come for me to start using a pair and get out on the bike. One glitch, however: I haven't actually sat on a bike (not one that's moving, anyway) for about eighteen months, since one March morning when my water bottle flew out of its holster and under the front wheel, sending me head-first onto the concrete without the faintest clue as to what had happened. I was bruised and grazed across my face, leg and arm. The driver of the car following me was alert, and stopped fast; I was lucky, and healed quickly. But the fear? That remained long after the scabs had faded.

I mention to Ren, my Commitment Aide, that I'm keen to do a long ride. In four weeks I'll be cycling some Carib-bean hills in between my swim and my run, and I need to build confidence. During the four or five years that she has been triathlon-training, Ren has done a lot of weekend cy-cling. She'll know the typical day-trip routes. All I'll need to do is follow, which means I can focus solely on training my cycling legs. They aren't completely defunct – I've be-gun attending indoor cycling classes – but there's a marked difference between riding on a stationary bicycle for forty minutes and hitting the roads for several hours.

'I know it's probably not what you want to do on a Sun-day morning . . .' I start.

'It's no problem,' she replies. 'I need to get a long ride in anyway. What about Box Hill?'

'Box Hill?'

'Yep. I know a route there and back. Around ninety kilometres in total.'

'Ninety kilometres? Really?' I gasp. 'That's quite a lot, don't you think?'

'Harden the fuck up, Fry,' is all she says. 'Just harden the fuck up.'

The day finally comes for our long ride. We decide to leave early, almost as soon as it gets light. The idea is that by the time I get home I'll have covered double the cycling distance required of me in an Olympic triathlon (and four times that of a sprint). Surely that will build some confidence, even if I won't be doing the swim and run today as well?

There are a few things, explains Ren, that I will need on any long ride: gas canisters to inflate tyres in an emergency, inner tubes in case of punctures, a special cycling T-shirt which has pockets in the back, and lastly what she calls 'baggies' in which to carry money, phone and keys to protect them from rain, sweat or both.

I don't have a single one of those, I admit, promising to at least buy plastic freezer 'baggies' from the supermarket, despite the fact that I can't understand why, if you're already carrying a rucksack, you would need them to protect your stuff. I also don't know how to change a puncture, which Ren insists is a pretty key thing to be able to do, especially if you're out riding on your own.

When I dare to suggest that I'm feeling a little anxious about the whole thing, she says: 'Stop getting nervous! It's a social(ish) ride, not the fucking Tour!'

We both decide it's best if Ren navigates ('Can't trust you bloody creative types,' she says) and that she should ride over to my place to pick me up at 8 a.m.

Tick tock. Eight fifteen and still no sign of Ren. Maybe she overslept? Eight twenty-five and she's not here. Perhaps she's had a crash? Eight thirty a.m. and –

The doorbell goes.

'Good afternoon,' I joke, opening the door.

'Does one need a passport to come this far south?' she exclaims, dragging her bike through the front door. 'I got a little lost.'

As she speaks, my nostrils are hit with the stench of pure alcohol.

'Were you out last night?' I ask, passing her a cup of coffee.

'I might have been,' she says.

'Have you had enough sleep? Are you OK to ride? Do you need food or . . . anything?'

I'm half hoping that she'll relent and we can call the whole thing off, blaming it all on Ren's hangover rather than my nerves.

'No, I'm Irish,' she says, and that, it seems, is that.

We move on to what to bring. Despite having none of the things Ren has told me I'll need, I've still got an awful lot of stuff.

'You don't take a rucksack on a long ride!' she laughs, not even trying to cover up her disdain.

Every time I've ridden anywhere – even just around Richmond Park – I've always taken a little rucksack, to hold my wallet and other essentials. Now I've lovingly packed snacks, an extra T-shirt, jumper, socks, camera and even a notebook, all of which come out of the bag after an unsuccessful effort by me to get them approved by Ren. The only thing that goes in the pockets at the back of the cycling top Ren has lent me is a plastic bag containing money and keys, my phone and an energy gel.

This is starting well, I think, with more than a little sarcastic amusement.

'Watch out, coffee gives me motor mouth,' says Ren, draining her cup and smacking its base down on the table. 'Right. Let's go.'

We start slowly, as I've warned Ren that I'm still getting used to the feel of the road bike with twenty gears and drop-down handlebars that's been kindly lent to me by a friend for the duration of my challenge. It weighs about the same as a pair of boots and moves along the road smoothly, making a purring sound as it goes. Because it's so fast, it feels anything but stable. Most disconcertingly I'm wearing my new cycling shoes, which clip into the pedals via small cleats under the soles. When you push your heel to one side, the cleat makes a clacking sound and attaches itself to the purpose-made pedal (you have to buy those too) so that you can't get out unless you yank your foot to the outside again. Almost every triathlete I've ever met – of any level – either cycles in clip-in shoes or is graduating to them soon. It's not compulsory but it is cool and, once you get used to it, comfortable. Or so the lady in the bike shop told me earlier this week when I started fiddling with a bright white pair on the shelf. I'm told that the real purpose behind these shoes (and the reason that I absolutely *have* to buy a pair) is to allow the rider to pull up on the pedal as much as they push down, so incorporating the hamstrings and glute muscles as much as the quadriceps on the front of the thighs. Some people say this gives a smoother ride. Others say it makes you faster, precisely because you can use more muscles. And some people say it makes you a 'real' cyclist.

What few people dwell on (but everybody knows), however, is that it's common to have a flurry of minor falls in the process of getting used to clipped-in cycling. And, sure enough, we are pulling up to a red traffic light near Merton Park when the real humiliation begins. I start to slow down, duly unclip the right foot and place it on the ground. Or, at least, that's what I should have done, but instead I don't pull my foot away hard enough and start to lean left before I can take either foot out of the pedals and suddenly I'm lying on my left side, the bike still attached to my feet and Ren's laughter ringing in my ears.

'Oops,' I say, and shift myself back up to standing.

I feel nothing but embarrassment right now but later, when I get home, I'll find a long bloodied scratch on the back of my right calf.

'Oh that's fucking made my day,' yells Ren. 'Brilliant! Just brilliant!'

And the light goes green. We're off again. I try to ignore the sinking feeling in my gut.

Half an hour passes. We cycle cycle cycle. I notice a few 'serious' cyclists (you can always tell because they have such a confident riding style and are dressed exactly like Ren, covered head to toe in wick-away fabrics) clocking my borrowed T-shirt as they ride past. They look at me with eyebrow-raising respect, combined with puzzlement that I'm moving as slowly as I am. I look down and notice, for the first time, a big red 'IM' emblazoned across the front.

IM = Ironman. It's the ultimate achievement in triathlon, as well as a major international brand. The simple act of completing an Ironman gives you kudos, long before any discussion of finishing times takes place. It's a word that pops up everywhere, once you start to become aware of it. This winter, the press are reporting madly on Gordon Ramsay's appearance at the world's most famous Ironman, Kona, in Hawaii. But more consistently and seriously, it's four-time Ironman World Champion, Britain's very own Chrissie Wellington (now retired), who's been making head-lines.

'Hey, Ren!' I ask, next time we stop. 'Did you do an Ironman by any chance?'

She races off ahead and ignores the question. A few minutes later we stop at another set of lights, where the sign clearly indicates the A240 to Kingston.

'Is that A240 or 340?' she asks, squinting.

I laugh. 'Um, 240. You blind or something?'

'Yes, as a bat,' she says, with a nonchalance that makes my blood run cold.

[28]

I start to ask about contact lenses.

'Oh no, I can't put anything in my eyes,' she baulks, as the light turns green and she whizzes off.

This woman is far crazier than I originally thought. Hungover, sleep-deprived, short-sighted (as I am, but obviously like normal people I employ corrective measures, especially when I'm out amongst fast-moving vehicles), and yet Ren still describes our five-hour ride into the Surrey hills and back as a 'nice way to wake up'.

For the next two and a half hours I try, quite simply, to remain alive and uninjured as we ride across miles of roads, out through Esher, Cobham and Stoke d'Abernon. At one point we end up on what must be an A road, if not a full-blown motorway. This time Ren, who is quietly sensitive to my anxieties, although desperately keen not to appear as such, warns me of what's coming.

'Now we're about to hit a main road here. Keep your knickers on, you'll be fine. Remember the cars don't actually want to hit you.'

I nod and steel myself.

The cars don't want to hit you.

Really? You could have bloody well fooled me, I think, overwhelmed by the sound of revving engines as they zoom past at around 60 mph. The sharp buzz that follows, like a supersized fly, creates a strong vibration that moves through my body and ignites my adrenal glands into action.

In the distance, there is just one constant: Ren on her

bike, moving steadily onwards, legs going around with the same gentle cadence, as if cycling down an empty lane on the way to a country pub in her home town of Limerick.

'Are we nearly at Box Hill?' I ask once we're reunited at a roundabout that takes us onto a slightly quieter road.

'Fuck no,' she laughs, as if I've said the stupidest thing she's ever heard. 'Now get on my wheel and suck up some air. We're gonna put the hammer down.'

We press on, at least another ten kilometres. Although it's beautiful today, it isn't remotely warm and after two hours of solid cycling I haven't broken a sweat. I don't feel thirsty in the least, but I know it will catch up with me.

'Can we stop a second?' I yell out. 'I think I should hydrate.'

'Sure.' Ren screeches to a halt and passes me a bottle. After sipping I offer it back, but she declines: 'I'm like a camel,' she says, adding: 'When you get home, take that peak off your helmet or we'll never go riding together again.'

Peak? It's only then that I notice her helmet doesn't have that detachable plastic bit jutting out from the front of it. As we near our destination, more and more cyclists are around us and none of them have peaks on their helmets either.

So here we are, finally. A big green sign marks the National Trust spot: Box Hill, at the bottom of the winding incline that will take us to the summit of Surrey's North Downs. It takes about seven minutes to climb at relaxed pace, and once at the top we are met with endless expensive bikes (mostly left unlocked), the clatter of cleats against concrete and a cafe serving the biggest slices of cake I've ever seen.

Immediately Ren bumps into a woman she knows from

her tri training club ('tri-hards' Ren calls them, and herself) and the conversation turns to missed pool sessions and which events they are considering doing next year.

'I'm having the season off,' says Ren's friend. 'So I'll just do a couple of friendly Half Ironman races. Nice courses. Not many people. That sort of thing. Just for fun.'

I splutter a little on my slab of date and chocolate cake.

Ren announces to her friend that yes, she'll be doing a swim session tonight. Her friend nods. So, a ninety-kilometre ride, followed by a short rest and then a pool session which, no doubt, will involve many lengths of front crawl, clearly seems entirely normal amongst these women.

'Is this what all triathletes do, or just those who take on the more extreme distance events?' I ask.

'Most tri-hards train twice a day,' Ren says.

Her friend nods.

'Oh brave new world,' I mumble, chewing on my cake with a sense of gathering doom.

Two and a half hours later I'm turning one final corner into my road as the winter sun drops down to virtually nothing behind the horizon. I feel weather-beaten, my skin burning from hours spent in the cold, and my back muscles are screaming and tight. It's a common by-product of hours spent bent double over handlebars and, I'm hoping, nothing some hot tea, toast, a bath and some rest can't sort out. The thought of that toast makes me salivate. I lean my bike against a wall – any wall – and collapse. My hips are sore and won't flex easily; my upper arms feel like they've absorbed the shock of ninety kilometres' worth of bumps and humps in the roads; even the soles of my feet are tender from being strapped into tight cycling shoes for over five hours.

On the table is strewn all the discarded kit that I had packed so cautiously, none of which I have even thought about since that initial desire for a jumper nearly six hours ago. I try to hop from foot to foot, wondering how it might feel to run right now, still saddle-sore, leg muscles seizing up from hours of riding. Not great, is the answer, but hey, I've just done four times the distance that I'll be required to cycle in my first triathlon. And yes, my body hurts all over, but who cares? I'm victorious! It wasn't really that hard, was it? I vaguely recall falling over at the lights, and struggling a little up some of the hills, but the cake, the banter and the brilliant view atop Box Hill are what remains.

4

By early November, I am both fitter and more freaked out. I've set aside the first three quarters of this month for research, both online and in the field, as per my recent cycle ride with Ren. Then, during the last part of November, I'll fly across the Atlantic to complete my first event. This will also be part of the research phase, and will give me a deeper understanding of what I'm facing so that, come Christmas, I can begin to plan next year's events and create a structure tough enough that I'll stay challenged and interested, but relaxed enough that I can keep some semblance of internal balance.

The research period starts with excitement and anticipation but quickly plummets into dead ends and despondency. Soon after reading *The Sports Gene*, a book exploring the science and genetics of athletic performance, I decide to email its author, David Epstein.

Is there a general consensus on what constitutes an ideal triathlete's body? I ask. Is it possible to be naturally built for swimming *and* running, for example? No, apparently not. 'The ideal body type for swimming is a long torso and short legs, whereas it's the opposite for running,' he writes. Given my long legs, I feel a little better about my hatred of swimming.

Is it actively counterproductive in fitness terms to train for both? I ask Epstein next. No, he replies, as one might rightly expect: 'Aerobic capacity (or VO2 max, a commonly-used measure of fitness referring to the maximum amount of oxygen that one's body can use and transport around itself, during exercise) is clearly transferable across all endurance sports. So an athlete who has high VO2 max trainability will have better endurance no matter what the medium.'

In essence swim training may make you a fitter person, which carries over to some extent into your running fitness. But that's where the carry-over ends. Because if having a long torso and short legs means you're likely to be good at the swimming part, it will have the opposite effect on your running. One's genetic strength in triathlon might automatically become one's genetic weakness and they can therefore work against each other in the very same race. Isn't that a bit like pressing the brake and the accelerator at the same time? Maybe it's this push–pull element that keeps people beguiled by the sport. The very essence of triathlon. It's what keeps people coming back, time and again, for more.

Days of staring at triathlon websites have left me feeling overwhelmed, sick and strangely angry. Why is there so much information out there? Where do I start? And how do I know who to trust? Most of all, why did anybody think it would be a good idea to put three different sports into one and make it a whole new sport of its own? Whoever it was, they must have been really, really bored. Even the beginner programmes I've viewed online seem to have a lot of sessions shoved into one week, many of which involve chlorination, something called 'turbo training' and, it seems, bricks.

Bricks?

Do they wear them in pockets, like weights? Throw them at each other in transition? I think it's a metaphorical reference to building blocks – the layering of one discipline atop another – but in any case I'm too distracted to really care. Because I've stumbled across a few negative reports of the swim section and am now fixated on the mass start – the bit where everybody dives into the water together.

Swimmers were crawling all over each other, says one blogger of her recent triathlon experience.

My mind conjures an image of ravenous insects, kicking, bumping and crushing one another, hungry to get the prize. And now, every time I close my eyes at night, I think about lining up with hordes of people behind me, in front of me, to the side of me . . . all pushing forward to the water's edge, until SPLASH! We all jump in and it's smack and thwack and bam. Can't breathe. Game over. Bye-bye.

That's not so irrational really, is it? I know of the power of water, second-hand, since both my brother and sister have had near-death experiences, one in the sea and one in a fast-flowing river, and I respect it even more as a result. That said, there is a point where a rational fear takes on irrational proportions, where the actual chance of an accident is far overshadowed by the assumed chances of one, and that, I think, is what's happening here. If I'm honest, it's been happening for a while and has begun to limit my options, stopping me, for example, from pursuing a dream of learning to surf, or ever (apart from this August, with Becky and Harry) swimming further than fifty metres out to sea.

Is it the cold? I wonder. Unlikely: even in summer triathletes are kept warm thanks to British Triathlon Federation rules, which state that the minimum water temperature at which wetsuits become optional is fourteen degrees centigrade.

Is it the fact that there aren't any lanes? Doubtful: the expanse of water on either side should make it less frightening, not more.

It must be the crowds. The claustrophobia, the insect effect of people 'crawling all over each other'. I must be tough, but right now, I feel anything but.

I'm actually so freaked out by it all that I think, fleetingly, of giving up before I've begun. Instead, I start asking around for help and, in mid November, just two weeks before the St Lucia Triathlon, I find myself in the Hospital Club in central London sitting across a table from triathlon coach Rob Popper.

Here, I hope, I've found my Tri Guide. I've sought him out because he's one of only twenty-eight Level 3 British Triathlon Federation coaches resident in the UK. Since there's no Level 4, that means he's fairly awesome at his job and can, quite possibly, come to my rescue. I've also heard his client base is forty per cent female, which, considering that us girls (according to the British Triathlon Federation) currently make up around a quarter of the triathlon-attacking public, suggests that his methods work particularly well for women.

Almost immediately I can see why he might make a good coach and especially why he might appeal to more nervous novice triathletes. Rob is incredibly unintimidating. When we meet he is dressed far more smartly than me in a polo shirt, jeans and jacket, rather than in the triathlete's Lycra uniform I was expecting. He's easy-going, soft-natured, and speaks in a lovely, lilting tone, with a subtle American accent. After a few minutes, I realise that he wears his ability and success much like a birthmark; he knows it's there, he tries vaguely to cover it up, but if it shows he is totally cool with it. Maybe that's because he's forty-eight, has had various (and varying) careers before this one, and spent much of his younger years heavily involved in martial arts. Or maybe it's just that his job involves dealing with neurotic, over-questioning beginners like me on a daily basis. He's done an Ironman himself, and all the stepping stones along the way. I get the impression that if Rob ever felt he had anything to prove then it's been proven and now he's here, just as he is. What begins as a straightforward chat about the sport quickly becomes a more philosophical discussion about its meaning. The three-in-one nature of triathlon, time-consuming, rigorous and challenging as it is, can help people get closer to the very essence of who they are, Rob suggests.

'My theory,' he says, 'is that there's a deep part of us that we're always trying to reconnect with – of just physical existence. Look at all these post-apocalyptic films . . . the end of the world has come on us, whether it's a zombie apocalypse or a disease or something like that. It comes down to: what kind of a person are you, deep down inside? Take away all this technology, take away all the banks and money and this and that . . . how would you survive, as a human animal? And in some ways it's interesting because most of these things are about stripping away the shreds of civilisation that we cloak ourselves in and finding out what's inside.'

It would be easy to draw some trite conclusions about why women are wanting to do away with their iPads and high heels and throw themselves instead into the wacky world of triathlon. What does seem more meaningful to note, however, is that there are differences in how the two genders approach triathlon training, particularly when it comes to the tougher, longer distances. The more masculine approach is to just hammer out the training sessions, going it alone until you break something, bounce into a different sport or burn out completely.

Rob says that women tend to do it differently: 'There's a huge groundswell coming up from women in the world of triathlon and particularly women who want to do their training properly. Women pay better attention to technique and are much better at listening to themselves and taking feedback.'

I sit back and bask in the glory of my entire gender – except that perhaps in terms of triathlon I am more like the stereotypical male athlete Rob mentions. The only communication I had with Rob prior to this meeting involved filling in lots of forms about my lifestyle, current training regime and goals, and a series of emails wherein he urged me to 'start slowly' and 'maybe think about two or three, rather than six to eight, triathlons in your first ever season'.

My immediate thought when I received this was, of course: *How ridiculous! Maybe I'll do a Half Ironman off the*

bat and teach him never to patronise me again. This is a typi-
cally male approach, though thankfully not one I've actually
carried out. I do, however, drop into conversation that I'll
be doing the St Lucia Triathlon in two weeks with virtually
no triathlon training whatsoever behind me. I've chosen a
shortish distance and I'm banking on a decent level of general fitness getting me round.

Rob half smiles. At least I think that's what he's doing. He
doesn't say much about it though, which worries me. Perhaps I'm being ridiculous, thinking I can just turn up and
swim, bike and run my way around a tropical island without
any proper kit or any idea of what I'm doing.

Clearly this whole idea of women being less bulldoggish
about triathlon, and similar extreme challenges, doesn't apply to me. But it does seem to have legs, so to speak. It's a
notion I've heard before, from Michael Lemmel, the organiser of the SwimRun championship Ötillö. This infamous
event is held annually in Sweden and involves teams of two,
in which each member completes seventy-five kilometres,
made up of ten kilometres swimming and sixty-five kilometres running between and over twenty-six islands. Every
year, many of the participants don't finish the event due to
stringent time caps along the way. Most of those people,
Michael explains in an email, are men:

In a race like Ötillö, men tend to enter races without thinking
of the consequences and the amount of training needed. They
have an attitude where they of course can manage. Women
on the other hand tend to think that they cannot manage even
though they are overqualified. If they then decide to enter they

prepare extremely well. During the race this is very clear. Men start off at a pace they cannot keep, often resulting in burning out. Women start at a pace they can keep the whole way. In short a more humble approach to the task at hand.

In the 2013 Ötillö event only forty of the 228 competitors were women. One of those forty women was Ren, competing in a team with a friend who only does Ironman races and no other type of triathlon. During our ride out to Box Hill Ren mentioned that she had met a couple of male marine reserves during Ötillö. The night before the race they had insisted it wouldn't be much of an issue for them to finish. The following day they dropped out halfway through.

I tell Rob about Ren and her performance at Ötillö. He nods and adds that nowadays any clear lines differentiating male and female approaches to training are getting blurred, with more men listening to what he calls his 'sensible coaching' and more women enjoying the 'flat-out, eyeballs popping, high-intensity effort that just feels great'.

Flat-out? Eyeballs popping? I've gone to that place before, when running, on a spin bike and during CrossFit sessions. But can I go there during swimming and cycling too? And, most importantly, can I do so from a place of self-acceptance rather than *not good enough*? Maybe it's not possible for anyone; perhaps to push oneself so far beyond one's comfort zone must require a degree of self-hatred. Or maybe it's just not possible for me. Certainly in the past I've set personal bests with a punishing voice in mind. The stick rather than the carrot. But the stick has consequences, more profound than the feel-good effects of having outdone oneself again.

I don't want to rely on a negative bias any more. It's self-perpetuating and painful. If I believe myself fundamentally not good enough, then any achievement disproving this belief will surely be short-lived? It's like treating the symptom and not the cure. It's taken me thirty-something years to get to this point, but the truth is that I've had enough of that damned stick.

5

Ten days later at Hewanorra International Airport, waiting for my bag to appear, I can feel my energy levels dropping, further and further towards the floor. 'It's only Tuesday evening though,' I try to reassure myself. 'The triathlon isn't until Saturday.' That should be plenty of time to get over jet lag, acclimatise to the heat, try out some sea swimming and find myself a bike.

During the taxi ride from the airport to my hotel we drive past vast banana plantations and through villages where children play on front porches whilst adults sit in the shade. A little later, we are slowed by thick traffic, and grind along a single carriageway in the capital, Castries, at no more than 2 mph.

'Rush hour,' the driver says.

I check my watch. He's right; it is 6.30 p.m., but, flanked by a cruise ship on one side and a bustling local market on the other, it's not exactly the kind of rush hour I'm used to. In London, there would be hundreds of cyclists buzzing around, jostling for space in their tiny blue lane. This drive has taken us almost the whole length of the island along some fairly well-tarmacked roads and yet I haven't seen a single cyclist. As for swimmers – on the coastal parts of the route I've seen only lily-white bodies, more than likely tourists taking a dip in the warm azure waters. I have, however, seen at least two people running, both men (the only woman I see taking exercise is powerwalking), legs moving fast and efficiently, taut muscles winking in the twilight.

This doesn't seem like a place burgeoning with fitness fanatics or wannabe triathletes readying themselves for the island's inaugural race. But who am I to talk? I'm a rookie myself. I can't even control my own imagination; the journey gives me far too much time to envisage strange Caribbean fish gnashing at my feet, or a 50-kilogram bicycle with a basket on the front and no gears to speak of.

Next morning, after seven hours' sleep, I wake feeling more positive. Saturday's triathlon will be fine – could be better than fine, in fact: I'm only aiming for completion of the sprint distance, after all. How hard can it really be? Fairly hard, is the answer that comes back. I'm fit and strong, but also jetlagged and injured. I've never swum seriously in my life (my technique is still terrible), barely cycled recently (apart from my big trip with Ren) and not been able to run (thanks to that damned injury) for nearly two and a half months.

The first thing I do is head down to the hotel pool clutching my swim cap and goggles. A morning swim is non-negotiable today, especially since there's no commute, it's warm both outside and in the water and the tinkling of cutlery makes the reward of breakfast feel that much closer. And while swimming still feels unnatural to me, there's definitely a fresh sense of purpose now that I have a motive for improving (i.e. Not Dying in the Triathlon).

After a few minutes I decide I'm ready to try the sea, and ask a member of staff to just keep an eye out as I head off for what can't be more than a hundred metres, max, to a small anchored boat and back.

I make it about halfway before turning around.

'Ey! What happen to you? You don't go anywhere!' asks my impromptu lifeguard in a thick Caribbean accent, when I reappear on the beach.

I had hoped he wouldn't notice.

'Suddenly got afraid of sharks,' I say sheepishly, although the seaweed and murky water had a lot to do with it as well, and explained, perhaps, why nobody else was in the sea.

'No sharks here!' he laughs, making me feel very stupid indeed.

I notice the boat out of the corner of one eye, marker of my failure, my cowardice, my stupidity.

'I'll try again later,' I promise.

But I don't – in fact I never set foot in that particular bit of sea again, because from that morning onwards, all the action takes place twenty minutes' drive away, at a luxury apartment complex and yacht mooring area called the Landings. It's here, against the beautiful backdrop of Pigeon Island and on the soft, white sand of Rodney Bay, that the triathlon and the various warm-up events will take place.

One of those events is an aquathlon. It's a generic term referring to a swim–run combination of any number of parts and any variation of distances, but tomorrow's aquathlon is a nifty four-hundred-metre swim, followed by a 1500-metre run.

I sign up immediately – this is the perfect opportunity to practise distance swimming, to prove to myself that I won't sink, give up or resort to (the ultimate no-no) breaststroke at any point. Early next morning, I turn up on the beach, milling about among the small field of people who've entered.

Officials draw our race numbers in waterproof ink on our arms. Number 8. That's me. I can't stop looking at the bold black squiggle across my tricep.

We rush into the water together and I get a taste of the splash and spray created by triathletes as they set off. It's a good introduction though; I feel entirely safe, able to hang back or go wide if I want. It's a short swim by triathlon or open water swimming standards but – maybe it's the jet lag, the oily Caribbean stew I hoovered down last night or the fact that these are race conditions – it doesn't feel quick to me. Thankfully, the second half is an improvement on the first; after about two hundred metres, I find myself alone and in a rhythm. I swim freestyle for about twenty strokes at a time before needing to stop and look around. My arms have relaxed, the salt water makes me more buoyant than I would be in a chlorinated pool and every time I tilt my head to breathe I see only the crinkling waves and a race steward, wandering along the sand away from the crowd.

'Go on, Lucy!' she yells in a Bristol accent so incongruous in these surroundings that I cannot help but hear it loud and clear. 'You're doing brilliantly! Keep it up!'

For a moment, I think I want to marry her. Then the silence returns; that thick sound of underwater nothingness. I can hear only my brain ticking away. What about Saturday? it demands: if I find *this* difficult, how am I going to cope with almost twice this distance? And – my mind shoots forward into the future – what about next year, when I'll have to do nearly four times this distance, in an Olympic triathlon?

*Whether you think you can, or whether you think you can't,
you're right*, I think, remembering some words spoken by
Henry Ford.

I think I can. I think I will. And – guess what? I do. It's
important: today marks a small shift (more of a curve in the
road than a turning point) in my relationship to swimming.
Not just this, but in my relationship to myself. I've coaxed
myself with the carrot rather than the stick; even if I never
become an exceptional swimmer I still want to learn to get
better at it. I want to feel for long periods of time the way I
felt for a few strokes in August, in between Palm and Union
islands, and the way I've felt in longer spurts here in St Lucia, three months later.

I'm well behind, but not quite last, as I step out of the
water, slightly dizzy, and make my way up the beach. The run
is done barefoot in swimming costume and, in my case, because I completely forgot to take them off, swimming hat and
goggles. The occasional fishing boat drifts past in the distance
and the land mass of Martinique hovers some fifty miles away.
But despite the perfect scene it's tougher than I expected, running up and down between flags on sand, especially directly
after swimming. Warm sand cakes my feet. Further up the
beach the finish-line banners ruffle audibly in the sea breeze.

'It worked! It worked!' I yell to a male stranger the minute
I've finished the race.

He looks blankly back, raising an eyebrow. I realise that,
in an endorphin-fuelled haze, I'm clutching my breasts for
emphasis, and quickly explain:

'Sorry, um, I was testing out the sports bra in the water.
Never mind.'

It's hardly something this slim gentleman could understand, but deciding what to wear for your first triathlon (or aquathlon) is a major conundrum if you have breasts. I'm told that everything is easier here in St Lucia because we don't need wetsuits; the water is warm and we can just pop a T-shirt and shorts over our swimming costumes for the ride and run. But, unlike elite athletes who tend to have such low body fat levels that they are virtually flat-chested, I still have breasts. They're not gargantuan, but neither are they insignificant, and I don't much fancy the party that's going to go on in my chest region if I'm not wearing a sports bra, especially for the run.

A brief search online before leaving the UK revealed that even if I do buy one of the waterproof all-in-one numbers worn by triathletes (either on their own in hot climates or under wetsuits in colder weather), it won't have anything other than minimal support, the kind of inner lining that's more useful for holding keys than D-cup breasts. Then, during my first day here in St Lucia, I encountered Paula. Another Londoner who had travelled out for a triathlon-focused holiday, she had cut out the inner layer of her trisuit that's designed for support ('because it's utterly useless if you have big boobs') in order to wear a sports bra underneath instead. We mulled it over for a while and decided it would be best not to wear a bra with a gap around the cleavage, as water would enter and drag us backwards, but instead one that meets in between the breasts.

It has worked well enough today. One more worry ticked off for Saturday. But I can't help feeling that it's not the best long-term solution. Paula tells me she has written to manufacturers asking why triathletes with larger breasts are alienated in this way and requesting they make a suit with better support. But she's never had an answer. We both agree it must be possible to create breast support in racing wear, so clearly this is a demand issue. When it's assured that tri-suits with an inbuilt sports bra will sell, the manufacturers will make them. But (a bit like women-only triathlons which always seem to involve events of less than Olympic distance) this is a chicken-and-egg situation. Women need to shout louder, to insist that those of all body shapes can be sporty, and that we can, in fact, go the distance just as readily as men.

Before I know it, Friday afternoon arrives and with just sixteen hours between me and my first triathlon, I am standing outside the Landings, looking out across the horizon. I've just raced a pink tropical sunset back across the 6.5-kilometre loop that will form the cycle portion of tomorrow's triathlon. Now, watching the skyline disappear into the dark, I breathe one very deep sigh of relief: it was a close call but I have wheels for tomorrow, borrowed from a local property manager who appeared to collect his daughter's road bike rather serendipitously as I was trying – and failing – to rent a working bike from a sleepy man at the inappropriately named Bicycle World (it's more like a run-down shack). I also have cleated shoes that fit the road-cycling pedals. Again, they are borrowed from the property manager's daughter and, although they don't fit my feet well, they do still fit. Just. So Cinderella will be going to the triathlon after all.

Now all I need to do is return to my hotel, eat, rest and organise my things for the race. Something at the bottom of my stomach starts to grumble. By the time I get back to my room I'm confined to the bathroom for an hour. I'm too nauseous to eat dinner, but manage a banana that – no more details, I promise – exits my stomach almost immediately, leaving me dehydrated and weak. In between loo trips I lay out all I'll need for tomorrow's race: swimming costume, swimming cap and goggles; helmet, energy gels, sunglasses, shorts and T-shirt, cycle shoes; trainers, headband and water for the run. And a race belt with my number – 66 – attached; it must be on the back for the ride and swivelled around to the front for the run. Most important of all, my alarm is set for 5.30 a.m. I need to get up, try to eat something, check out of my hotel and step into a taxi bound for the Landings, all by 6.15 a.m. so that I'm sure to be there for quarter to seven, an hour and a bit before my race begins. Some earlier chatter with fellow participants about transition has left me on high alert and convinced I've forgotten something. I'm beginning to suspect that organisation and gear are as much part of triathlon as the actual sporting endeavour.

It's nine o'clock the night before my first ever triathlon and I am far from rested; far from prepared; far from confident. I clutch my stomach and lie in the foetal position hoping for sleep. Outside the rain is biblical, plummeting down furiously. If this happens tomorrow (entirely possible, since it's the tail end of the rainy season), especially during the ride, it's going to be carnage.

Ten minutes later, just nodding off, I'm roused by the sound of an incoming email. It's from Irish Ironman Ren, offering some last-minute advice. Blunt as ever, she writes:

Hey, good luck tomorrow and remember to attack the race:

1. Swim: go off the front, believe me, going off the back is way worse and you will endure far more violence. Going off the front with the better swimmers, they will avoid you and pass you quickly, leaving the frantic punchers behind you and out of your way. The field will spread in the first 100 m, get onto a pair of feet and draft. Remember, first out of the water rarely wins.

2. Bike: go hard or go home. There is no traffic on the roads and fuck the other riders. Get low and aero and onto a good solid gear where you can hit a cadence of 90 rpm. Spin hard and the speed will carry you.

3. Run: take the first 5 mins handy to settle your legs, then go for it. It is only 5K, easy. Dig deep, concentrate and hold your form and your leg will be fine.

4. Attack the transitions and don't worry about nutrition, you won't need to eat anything in a race that short. Stay hydrated and if you need to piss, just do it in your pants.

It's more than a little different from the text message I received a couple of days ago from tri coach Rob Popper, which I reread now, to calm my nerves:

Hey Lucy – things to bear in mind:

a) Don't overdo it in the aquathlon. Treat it as pure practice rather than a race.

b) Any other exercise you do, keep it short and sharp so you are race-ready (don't want to be really tired and you do want to be fast so think, sprint sprint sprint then rest, rest, rest).

c) Have fun, so ignore any of my advice in a or b that doesn't support c.

In the event, most of the advice, particularly Ren's, is either ignored or proves superfluous. There is, for starters, plenty of traffic on the roads (Ren has wrongly assumed that this will be a closed-road event like most in the UK). Plus, I don't really know what a 90 rpm cadence even feels like yet, and I don't have any intention at this stage of pissing in my pants. With a whole sea ahead, eighty-five of us at most jumping in together and four oversized buoys to aim for, there will be no need to (in Ren's words) 'endure violence'. Though there's certainly been some more violence in my stomach overnight, leaving me depleted before I've even begun and only able to ingest a sugary energy drink as pre-race breakfast after non-existent dinner the night before.

When I get to the start I sit quietly for five minutes on a rock as people mill about, bare feet sinking into the sand, adjusting swim caps, getting numbers written on their arms. My mouth is dry, my muscles lacking in energy. This is not how it was supposed to go, I think pitifully, coaxing my stomach to withstand the pressure and making it all sorts of promises – no oily food, no cheap meat, no curry, no coffee, ever again – that I will never keep.

I'm old enough to know that self-pity is cathartic for five minutes but useless much beyond that. Once I've had my moment, I look around for somebody to chat to. There are a handful of athletes from the neighbouring island of Martinique, all wearing trisuits over their defined, lithe bodies. They look so professional in fact that it's as if they have arrived at the wrong race; there might be only about fifty miles between the islands but the gap between these men and women and the St Lucian participants (excited, naïve, mostly doing their first triathlon) is far larger. It is, from what I gather, the result of the French government's continued funding of Martiniquais sporting efforts and a kind of support that St Lucians don't yet enjoy at all. The message, one could argue, is that money talks. Especially when it comes to a sport like triathlon, where the gear and time are costly.

It's then that I realise just how special today will be. If it's deemed a success and continues annually, then Tri St Lucia will no doubt attract more people, more professionals or more of the ambitious amateurs who will require staggered starts, with higher entry costs for limited spaces that will sell out quickly and prohibit many who wish to from participating. Today, because of its newness, there are plenty of first-timers; women who, like me, are unafraid of admitting to nerves, all of whom insist they'll be taking it easy, swimming off the back, going gingerly on the bike (and a number of other self-deprecating phrases and assertions of caution). But I'm struck by the high levels of gutsiness amongst both men and women, some more experienced, but most of us just here to challenge ourselves and give triathlon a go.

Just before the starting gun goes, I strike up a conversation with a Scottish lady. Resident on the island, she began learning front crawl from scratch just three months previously, yet she's one of the very few women here today to do the longest distance. If I didn't feel so washed out from the stomach bug I might wonder if I've been pathetic just entering the sprint.

But no time for regrets now – the gun cracks and we are off. I snuggle in somewhere near the back of the pack and start out easy. Anybody who has ever done a race of any kind will know that the bit immediately before it begins is usually the worst of all, and it's a relief to get started. The fact that I've swum (and survived) in these same waters yesterday during the aquathlon has worked wonders for my confidence. I feel safe and calm and try to focus solely on working up a rhythm: three strokes and breathe; three strokes and breathe; again, again, again, with as few stops to glance up and see where I'm going as I can manage. When I wade out of the water after 750 metres – with those doing the long course already well into their second lap – I feel relaxed, happy and composed.

I am, if I'm honest, a little too relaxed, too happy and too composed during transition, chatting away to marshals, drinking water, placing my helmet on and then casually swanning off on the bike and up, up, up, out towards an area called Cotton Bay. Along the route I pass several cyclists coming the other way, on the return portion of the lap (of which 'sprinters' like me must complete two, and the endurance junkies four); some of them are behind, having done two laps of the swim, and some ahead. It becomes impossible to know who is where but it's easy to pick out the more serious triathletes, their heads adorned with spacey go-faster helmets and their faces painted with a stony focus. I wave or yelp at most people. I'm delirious. Loving every second. My stomach and my hip are holding up. What isn't there to be cheerful about? Most of the British ladies I've met nod when we pass, or even smile and utter some words of encouragement; forty-three-year-old Paula was behind me at the start of the ride but is, I note with more than a little concern, quickly catching up. I try to console myself that the eleven years between us in age is counterbalanced by Paula's triathlon experience: this is her third sprint-distance event. But then there's fifty-one-year-old Melanie, also no stranger to triathlon and an ex-runner. She exits the water two minutes before me and adds another three minutes during the ride (crossing the line a full five before yours truly).

I would call it humbling. Ren would call it an arsewhipping. But despite it showing every bit of my inexperience, the camaraderie, at least, is welcome. The heat becomes more forceful with every passing minute and by 9 a.m. reaches around thirty degrees centigrade. What's more, the cycle ride is full of hills, steep enough in fact that the organisers have deemed 13.2 and 26.4-kilometre rides to be the respective equivalents of 20 and 40 kilometres of the flatter cycling usually involved in a sprint and Olympic-distance triathlon.

When I first saw that announced I scoffed: just a 13.2-kilometre ride, seriously? Surely you'd have barely got onto your bike before you were hopping off again. But the reality is very different. It's humid and, as I discovered yesterday, the top set of gears on the property manager's daughter's bike don't work, with those on the lower rung causing a portentous crunching sound whenever I make a change, followed by the repetitive clicking that I know to be the result of a gear chain in need of some realignment. The cleats on the shoes are set so loosely that with the slightest movement of a leg they can pop right off the pedal. There are also challenges on the road itself – though thankfully I remember from yesterday's trial run where these are situated – speed bumps, the odd pothole and a particularly hazardous ditch just at the bottom of the biggest hill.

By the second lap I'm tiring, just a little, a voracious thirst creeping up inside my throat and drying out my tongue. It feels as if I am pushing with all my might on the pedals, speeding down the final straight and back into transition, though somehow I'm still being overtaken on the bike. A big slurp of water, a change of shoes, an unbuckled helmet and I'm off, on two feet, for a five-kilometre run.

Then something awkward happens. My legs refuse to work properly. Picking one up, and then the other, in an action formerly known to me (quite well) as running, is suddenly ridiculously hard to execute. Where have I put my feet? They are smacking the ground but not bouncing back up. And where is my proud chest, my diligent attempt at the mid-sole strike advocated by so many decent runners? All of them have been replaced by a slumped, shuffling figure running about two minutes per mile slower than she usually would. What's more, up until now, however testing, this has been fun. But running immediately after cycling hard for around forty minutes?

Turns out that that's no fun at all.

What did Ren say? *Dig deep, concentrate, hold your form . . . and your leg will be fine . . .*

On the latter point, she is just plain wrong (it's definitely hurting again, but more of that later). Dig deep? I think I am. But I don't think I've moved into what triathletes often call the 'hurt locker'. I'm hardly holding my form, slumping forward and shuffling along as my body falls victim, with depressing predictability, to the heat and my lack of brick training in which (I've now learned, a little too late) the transition from bike to run is practised, over and over, until your muscles and mind know what to do. As for concentration? Fat chance; we may have begun by swimming in the Caribbean Sea but the shape of this island tip means that the run to Pigeon Island and back flanks the Atlantic Ocean, where surfers catch crests and my eye in equal measure.

It's not a bad thing though – the beauty of this scene instantly boosts my mood. I remind myself to appreciate it. It'll soon be over, I think, half relieved and half disappointed that this is true. And sure enough, around fifteen minutes later, I cross the finish line, jubilant.

Race Ambassador and former Great British Olympic decathlon champion Daley Thompson puts a medal around my neck.

'Enjoy it?' he asks.

I'm think I'm smiling too much to talk. I give the poor man a very sweaty hug.

'Yes,' I breathe. 'Yes and yes and yes, but . . . uh . . . I've . . .'

I've got a lot of work to do . . . The words don't come out. I'm bent double, inhaling oxygen. When I look up, ready to talk again, Daley has gone. He's a few metres away, putting a medal around another neck, and another and another, including Paula's. She crossed the line around three minutes behind me. We congratulate one another, our mutual joy tangible. For a while I hang about, munching on bananas and sipping water, cheering as the fastest of the long -distance participants start to appear. There's nothing better, once you've completed a challenge and are still high on the endorphins and an enormous sense of achievement, than encouraging others to finish their own.

One thought niggles at me: these triathletes have done double what I've done. Which is exactly what I've got to do next summer (technically more, in fact, due to the truncated cycling distances in Tri St Lucia). In theory, that sounds like plenty of time. Maybe, if it was just about completion – a one-off – I could lope around, whatever . . . but of course I want to do well, to find out what I'm capable of, to train hard and then even harder, for an event that could all go wrong at the last minute. That's just the nature of triathlon. It's just the way I think. And it's also, quite possibly, just a part of being human.

⟋⟍

That evening I travel to the south of the island via windy, unlit roads hugged by thick rainforest on either side. It is dark when I arrive at my hotel, an old cocoa plantation building that has been beautifully restored in deep brown wood, and I can make out little of my surroundings. I sleep fitfully, muscles twitching, whilst my brain dips in and out of watery dreams. When I wake, very early, and wander onto the balcony, the perfect curve of a rainbow shines back at me and into my tired eyes. In this area, such 'liquid sunshine' (as the locals call it) is a near-daily occurrence. But for me this morning, it holds a new message: triathlon is bright and beautiful, or at least it'll seem that way the morning after.

Already my greed is getting the better of me – whether it's the rainbow or the after-effects of triathlon, I want more. Before the muscle aches from yesterday's exertions have gone, I'm lying awake wondering if I could have done better, pushed harder, finished sooner. The swim, surprisingly, went as well as could have been expected – it took me around twenty minutes, which puts me at very slow but not dreadful, and, given my lack of experience, I'm feeling fairly hopeful. The cycle ride, on the other hand, took a very disappointing forty-one minutes. And as for the run? Well, I know for certain I could do better there: twenty-nine minutes, four or five minutes longer than I'd usually take to run that distance.

I remind myself that the run in a triathlon is, by its very nature, made difficult by what's come before. But in truth it wasn't just dead legs and a sickly stomach that held me back. I can admit to myself this morning that I gave in, just a little, to the pain.

It's your first triathlon after all, said Tired Voice. *Any time you set will be a personal best.*

Better to start low, haha, or you'll have nothing to improve on next year!

Just set a number, any number, to beat next time.

There is a difference between completing and competing (and yesterday I completed). The former involves a 'just make it round' attitude, whereas the latter takes focus, determination and an ability to push through a certain type of fairly excruciating physical pain. Competing, in this instance, needn't mean trying to do better than others in a race – though obviously it often does – it can also just mean beating one's own previous performance. It's a purpose, in and of itself. But purpose rarely exists within a vacuum. It must be encouraged through smaller goals making up an overall plan. If I want to compete rather than complete I need to get clear in my mind, and in my diary, just how these next nine months are going to go. Which events shall I do next? How shall I structure my training? What are my potential pitfalls, my obvious strengths? And can I do it all in a measured, unhysterical fashion?

On the latter, I suppose, only time will tell. In terms of plotting the remainder of my year in triathlon, however, there is much still to do. I start thinking first about what excites me. I want to get faster over sprint distance – to compete, albeit mostly with myself – as much as I want to complete over Olympic distance. The sprints will obviously help with training for an Olympic, but how many can I do without neglecting the longer endurance training necessary for the big one? And should I do one, or two, or even three sprints, along with one, or two, Olympic distance tris?

Only when I know what I'm working towards exactly can

I plan my training in exquisite detail and pore over it with a masochistic eye. For the first time since I set my triathlon challenge, I feel overwhelmingly excited about what's in store. Do other people feel like this after a race? Maybe it's just the perfectionist in me, the part that made my young self treat sports day with such seriousness and sets the bar higher, almost immediately, after it's been cleared. Or maybe it's that triathlon draws out this part of me, triggering my inherent sense of not being good enough. Does it attract this type of person – the egomaniac with an inferiority complex?

I begin writing furiously in my notebook, working backwards from next summer. It begins with goals, then goes back to what requirements I must meet to reach those goals. And then how I can meet those requirements – where is my starting point? The British triathlon season doesn't start for another six months and I'm itching to race sooner than that. The only option is to go abroad again but for that I'll need funds – currently non-existent.

The ideas percolate for a few hours, with no decisions properly made. Just as my brain is gearing up, my body sends a quick reminder that all's not well, as my hip hurts for the entire flight home. I feel uncomfortable wherever and however I sit. I want to get up and move all the time. But I also want to sleep. It aches from my lower back down to the outside of my lower leg. I worry about the damage I've done by running on it. I worry about the money any continuing physiotherapy is going to cost. Most of all I worry that it won't get better – that my triathlon dreams will be trashed.

6

After my first race I've returned to the UK both more inspired and more injured. Thankfully I met a fantastic physiotherapist whilst in St Lucia, who happens to work in south-
west London, not far from where I live. I visit him in early
December and he manages to properly diagnose the issue in
my leg. It is a locked sacroiliac joint, he explains, pointing
to a place at the side of my lower back near my hip, and it's
been sitting atop a nerve, causing that horrible, debilitating tugging sensation I've had down my leg. It could take a
while, he warns, but I will get better, provided I don't aggravate it with too much, too soon. Absolutely no running for
the moment, he instructs, and instead prescribes hundreds
of daily step-ups to strengthen my buttock muscles so that
they can help keep the joint in place.

Whilst my body may be stuck, I do at least now have a lot
more hope that it will mend. I'm also thrilled to be reunited
with Bella, though a little surprised at how uninterested she
remains in ever taking part in a triathlon. She tells me how,
despite my excited chatter and newfound enthusiasm, she
still thinks the whole thing sounds a little bit ridiculous, a
supreme effort to challenge oneself purely for its own sake.

'I know,' I tell her and laugh. 'It is! Completely ridiculous!'

But what was previously pejorative – ridiculous! – has
become a positive, almost without me noticing the switch.

When I see the word 'TRIATHLON' in my head it's now written in colour, drenched in tropical sunshine, and has a rainbow in the background. It might change when I do my first English triathlon under a grey and rainy sky, of course, or go double the distance with an Olympic-length event. We'll have to wait and see. Right now I'm excited and I want to drag my wife into it with me.

But she's not taking the bait. If I paid her a thousand pounds she might give it a go, she informs me with nonchalance. Until then? Fat chance.

Over the next few days I get a smattering of happy messages from those who understand the joy of having completed one's first event. Ren congratulates me on the loss of my triathlon virginity and on diving in despite the stomach upset. Rob asks for a written race report, presumably so he can figure out which areas I most need to work on and also hear about the new race on the warm-weather triathlon circuit. My newest friends, tri-couple Emily and Suzanne, to whom Stewie introduced me just before I left for St Lucia, also express their excitement at my having plunged headfirst into their favourite sport.

You're a triathlete now! they both exclaim.

Really? Am I? Ren and Rob have said exactly the same thing in both their messages. It's strange – unlike all other sports I can think of, triathlon only seems to require the completion of one event before you're an athlete of that sport and you've officially got the triathlete T-shirt. But, as I'm beginning to feel myself, for most the T-shirt isn't enough. It looks so good on that it might perhaps look even better when accompanied by the sweatshirt (another race) and then the trousers (a different, longer race), jacket (another) and endless pairs of shoes (another race, another event, another try). Wherever they go, they wear the outfit. It becomes a part of – or is – their identity.

There is nobody I've yet met for whom this is more true than Suzanne. Four years and four months before I completed my first triathlon – an ocean swim and hot, sticky cycle ride and run – Suzanne took part in hers, at the age of thirty-three, amid the rain and hills of England's Peak District. Strictly speaking, she wasn't entirely new to it; she had completed one short, women-only triathlon some years previously, back in her home country of New Zealand. However, it 'didn't really count', she explains to me over brunch one freezing December morning: 'I just waded through the shallow water; I didn't even bother to swim.' But in January 2009, spurred on by her little brother's recent completion of an Ironman triathlon, she decided if he could do it then so could she. Suzanne made a New Year's resolution that has changed her life forever: to complete the Ironman UK, in Bolton that July.

I have a brother too and I can identify with this *anything he can do* attitude, but I think perhaps that my competitiveness has limits that might stop around Half Ironman. But with just six months to prepare and money in short supply (since the entry fee alone was around £300), Suzanne began her journey. She bought an old second-hand bike and began cycling at weekends. She had no experience of real training so downloaded a programme from the internet. It was only when she arrived at weeks 13–15 that she realised there was a glitch and the programme was empty. Blank pages stared at her for the whole twenty-one days where training suggestions were meant to be.

Suzanne plodded on. She knew nothing about interval training so just did 'lots and lots of volume' – endless lengths, long steady runs and rides. When she began swimming in her local pool, she could only manage four lengths – one hundred metres – without stopping. The Ironman would require her to swim thirty-eight times that distance, in open water.

She kept on going and, quickly, the distances built up. Her muscles grew and her stamina improved. She made her own sports drinks (regular squash, diluted with water and a teaspoon of salt) and ate a lot of creamed rice and cereal to keep her fuelled for long rides and runs.

During these six months, Suzanne also isolated herself, quickly discovering that when she told people about her intention – to go from woman to Ironwoman in just six months – she was inundated by negativity and fear. She'd done a marathon the year before and not faced any of the same 'Are you sure you'll manage it?' reaction. But something about Ironman scared people. It made them worry for her. Or for themselves. She wasn't sure. She continued, doggedly, to train, explaining to the few close friends who didn't react negatively why she was doing what she was doing. She would apologise to them for her temporary disappearance from their lives – whenever they wanted to see her she would be training – but explain that this was something she felt she really had to do. The ones who were important mostly understood, or at least accepted, the kind of physical and mental preparation involved in getting oneself to the start line of an Ironman triathlon. None of them, however, not even Suzanne herself, knew what it would take to finish the damned thing.

After weeks of training, the time came to practise open water swimming. She bought the cheapest wetsuit on the market and, with not long to go until the race, took four open water swimming lessons. As she crept into lake water for the first time, Suzanne's mind was full of trepidation and imagined horrors. She was convinced there were going to be bodies, or weeds, pulling her under. But she didn't drown as she had feared. In fact, she returned to dry land each time more confident than before. These swim sessions marked a steep but vital learning curve: she learned to rotate and reach, and gathered experience of what it felt like to swim in murky water, without the end of the pool to rest upon. Without those lessons, she insists, she might not have made it through the 3.8-kilometre Ironman swim within the cut-off time and thus never finished the race at all.

When the day of the Bolton Ironman came, however, the conditions couldn't have been worse for Suzanne. Storms the day before the event had left the course washed out by torrential rain. The transition area too was waterlogged, and there was no parking, so the many hundreds of athletes (along with their supporters) had to be transported by bus to the start area. It was the stuff of nightmares even for an experienced triathlete, let alone a first-time Ironwoman.

Many athletes waited in the lake, treading water, but

Suzanne stayed onshore until the gun went off, partly because the water was so cold and partly because she wanted the crowds to go on ahead. There were fourteen hundred competitors in the mass start, all going off together. It was a field of which no more than ten per cent were female, which meant smaller women, like Suzanne, might find themselves being swum over by men of twice their weight. It was safer, she thought, to start at the back of the pack and let the more competitive charge off. Not that Suzanne could just potter along, however: the swim had to be finished within two hours and twenty minutes, or else her race was over. But thankfully that practice paid off, and she exited the water in one hour and fifty-five minutes, with thighs like ice.

Her first conscious thought on reaching land again was what a long, long swim it had been. It was nothing, however, compared to her next challenge: a 180-kilometre bike ride in the infamously hilly Peak District, three laps of a sixty-kilometre course. Again a cut-off had been set and by the second lap she realised she was short on time. Everything would be all right so long as she didn't slow down too much or get a puncture.

By the end of the third lap she was exhausted. What's more, she hadn't got off her bike (not even for a pee) for the entire eight hours, five minutes and thirty-eight seconds that it had taken her to complete this brutal, undulating distance. The mud that had gathered around her shoes had become rock solid and glued her to the pedals, into which she had been clipped for the duration. Unable to dismount her bike when the time came, she fell sideways onto a chicken-wire fence and yelled for help from a nearby marshal.

Help came and Suzanne was freed from her congealed shoes. She took her cycling socks off and put her regular trainers on before starting to run, painfully, through transition. Fatigue was taking its toll and she was no longer thinking straight. Her socks? That smell. Her socks.

Her socks were in her mouth. She had no recollection of putting them there.

Darkness fell as Suzanne trudged through her marathon run, picking off other competitors, in high-visibility jackets, one by one by one. One foot after the other. Sometimes that was all that she could do. Just keep on keeping on. This was what she had worked so hard for over the last six months. Her entire social life had been on hold. Her weekends had involved nothing more than training, eating and recovery, and on weekdays she'd been up early to exercise and knackered pretty much all of the time.

Whatever happened in her body, and however desolate she felt, Suzanne just kept on going. She passed the halfway mark and then the thirty-kilometre mark. When she got to forty she knew it was almost over, and then, at last, Bolton town centre appeared, marking the final kilometre of the race. Still she couldn't see the line but the noise of a jubilant crowd kept getting closer until, finally, after five hours, thirteen minutes and six seconds of running, Suzanne finished her first Ironman triathlon.

The whole race had taken fifteen hours, thirty-three minutes and thirty-two seconds in total, and still it wasn't over. After every triathlon there's the obligatory return to transition to pick up one's bike, helmet and wetsuit, along with other paraphernalia, and this time all the competitors, their limbs twisted and angry from their exertions, had to catch a bus back to the start line. Suzanne then had to drive two hundred miles home from the Peak District to Staines. Her eyelids dropped a little too low on the motorway a few times, and she had to stop for a snooze at one point, but somehow she made it. Arriving outside her house at 6.30 a.m., she limped inside for a quick nap before work, leaving all the doors and the boot of her hire car open (which she still can't remember doing) and still arrived at work by 9 a.m.

As she continues with her story, I wonder: could I have done all that? I really don't think that I could. Sure, I like challenge and enjoy the blissful focus a really hard training session brings. But I'm almost a little surprised to say that I don't want to put myself through that kind of physical abuse. Perhaps if I had stumbled into the world of triathlon a few years ago, things might have been different. But for now I'm happy with sprint and Olympic distance, with biting off exactly what I think I can chew.

Is that self-preservation or cowardice? Perhaps it's neither. One woman's challenge is another woman's nightmare. For Suzanne, one Ironman, quite simply, wasn't enough.

The day after Bolton, her boss sent her home at 3 p.m. and that night she finally slept, sixteen hours straight. It was then that her body and mind began to process the scale of her achievement. After crossing the finish line of her first marathon the previous year, Suzanne had expected something to be different in some way. But it wasn't. This time, though, something had changed. An Ironman was different. Suzanne knew now that nobody could ever put her down again.

A week after finishing the Bolton event, Suzanne began wondering what improvements she could make. It's funny how that happens; I know from my own experience of running how we sit on our sofas and reflect on the glory of the finish line. We wonder what might be possible with better preparation, better kit or a little coaching. Quickly the memories of muscle burn disappear and the thought that 'I probably *could* go faster' arrives instead. Before you know it you've signed up for another event.

That's exactly what Suzanne did. The following year, having met and started dating her triathlete girlfriend, Emily, Suzanne became an Ironwoman all over again. This time it was in Nice in the south of France and, whilst the conditions were in huge contrast to those in Bolton, they were every bit as punishing. It was a heatwave, thirty-five degrees at times. The cycle route was extreme – essentially ninety kilometres uphill and another ninety downhill – and half of each of the four laps of the run course faced directly into the afternoon sun.

'That's hotter than St Lucia was,' I reflect, as she recounts this part of her tale. I remember feeling drained by the heat of the early morning. Suzanne had to deal with the burn of mid afternoon, along with a course that was more than eight times longer than mine.

But even a person as dogged as Suzanne isn't immune to nature's force. She kept herself as well hydrated as possible but her British summer training hadn't prepared her for this heat. Midway through the marathon, over fourteen hours into the race, her mind started playing tricks on her that outdid the sock situation the year before in Bolton. One part of Suzanne's boiled brain convinced another part that she'd forgotten how to speak English, and now could talk only in French. Over time, when she ran, she became upset and tearful, talking to herself in her rusty schoolgirl French, anxious about how on earth she would explain this to Emily when she finished. Who would believe her? And would she have to relearn English again? *Pourquoi moi?* she moaned.

Once night fell and the day's spectators departed, the final kilometres of the race seemed to stretch out forever. Suzanne's run turned into what's known in the triathlon community as the 'Ironman shuffle', her heavy footsteps scuffing against the hot tarmac. She saw the finish line in the distance and with fewer than twenty minutes to go until the cut-off time she was reunited with Emily in the finishers' area where, rather unexpectedly, she found herself speaking English.

I sit back in my chair, shellshocked. Despite the Christmas music playing on the restaurant's stereo, my mind is full of Peak District rain, French heatwave and scuffing feet. I look across at Suzanne's thirty-two-year-old girlfriend, Emily.

She smiles. She's clearly heard all this before.

'What's happened since?' I ask Suzanne.

'Oh, lots,' she says.

Both Ironman events were, to some extent, just the beginning of Suzanne's triathlon journey. Since the completion of Ironman Nice she's taken running lessons, ticked Ironman Austria off her list (thirteen hours eleven minutes) and represented her country as a non-elite 'age group' competitor in the 2013 International Triathlon Union Sprint Championships. The next twelve months or so, she tells me, is all mapped out. Firstly, there is the London Marathon, in April next year, which Suzanne hopes to complete in less than three hours and thirty minutes, explaining to me that this is an excellent way of preparing herself for an eleven-hour Ironman in future. Then, in May, she and Emily are heading over to the Stockholm archipelago to race together in the Utö SwimRun. This event, comprising 29.6 kilometres of running and 2.7 kilometres of open water swimming, is the qualifier for its big sister (double the distance): Ötillö, which Ren conquered earlier this year. Suzanne also hopes to take part in a couple of Half Ironman events in the summer, though these have yet to be finalised. In October, Suzanne and Emily together plan to swim the strait from Gibraltar to Morocco, which, depending on the tides, can range between sixteen and twenty-two kilometres.

'And what about you?' I turn to Emily.

I'm not sure I'm ready to be stunned again but thankfully Emily's story, though impressive, is ever so slightly less dramatic. Having leapt into the world of triathlon in 2008, Emily has been fairly fanatical ever since. This year she also has various challenges planned. Very soon after Suzanne has run the London Marathon, Emily will fly off to warm-weather training mecca Club La Santa in Lanzarote for a ten-day immersive triathlon training camp, which culminates in an Olympic-distance triathlon event. When she returns to the UK, she plans to take part in a ten-kilometre swim in the Lake District, a fourteen-kilometre swim around Henley and a triathlon at Eton Dorney Lake and, of course, to swim and run side by side with her girlfriend in Sweden in May.

No rest for this couple, it seems. Oh, and wait – they are

planning to do an Ironman together next December in Australia, in lieu of a civil partnership ceremony. Each to their own, I think (though personally I'd take a ceremony and a party over a long day of exercising in the Antipodean sun, any time), feeling strangely relieved to think that at least with these new conjoined goals on the horizon, Suzanne and Emily will get to spend more quality time together.

'We don't actually get to see each other that much,' Suzanne explains.

Emily works freelance as a sports coach, whereas Suzanne works regular office hours. Both swim at the Serpentine in Hyde Park, but Emily does so on a Tuesday, Wednesday and Thursday whereas Suzanne goes on Friday, Saturday and Sunday, so as to meet their disparate goals and suit their differing work schedules.

'Nobody at the Serpentine even knows that we're together!' Suzanne says.

'We used to have Friday date-night runs,' says Emily, sounding amused.

'Yes, we *did*! Remember that?' Suzanne says, pointedly.

Emily shrugs. 'What we did is . . . we'd run up Primrose Hill together. And we'd look down over the view of London, run the 5K back home, and have an ice bath.'

'An ice bath? How on earth is *that* romantic?' I laugh.

But apparently it was.

'We don't do it any more,' says Emily. 'We don't have time.'

Triathlon. It has brought these two together, but might it one day cause a rift? I realise now that I have developed mixed feelings about the idea of Bella doing a triathlon. The sport is already proving rather all-encompassing and I'm beginning to feel relieved, rather than frustrated, that I live with a person who isn't currently involved in it. Yet I also want to share the big events in my life with Bella; I fear becoming immersed in the sport as Emily and Suzanne have, and am concerned about what that might do to our relationship, should Bella choose to remain outside the whole world of triathlon. Will I become addicted, as so many triathletes do, to outdoing my own previous achievements? Will I want to test myself over longer and longer distances? Right now I can't ever imagine completing an Ironman, not so much because of its scale but more because I can't find within me any willingness to do it. A Half Ironman is plausible, just about. But there's something about Ironman . . . Four months into my year in triathlon and I've become convinced that were I to sign up tomorrow for the ultimate long-distance tri, my reasons for doing so would be more injurious than inquisitive. I remind myself that I no longer want to be driven by the stick, nor to beat myself towards glory.

7

Late December, and Christmas arrives, a time for swimming in movies and mincemeat rather than the pool; for cycling between sugar highs and lows rather than on roads; for running upstairs to wrap last-minute presents rather than outside around the local park. Except this year I choose health over hedonism and give my body no rest during the holidays. Ren is still training, hard, in between parties. Like a typical triathlete she views extra days off and fewer cars on the road as opportunities for a long ride. Huge plates of food mean surplus energy that can be utilised on a long run. Emily and Suzanne take a similar view. They are swimming, running and skiing their way around Hong Kong and Japan.

I'm a triathlete now, so I follow suit, slotting in six training sessions during Christmas week. Rob has already begun to mutter about how one crucial part of tri training is to practise one's transitions. He urges me to begin swimming in a wetsuit, and to add some cycle–run combination sessions.

I start with an attempt at a cycle ride. How long can I use the winter as an excuse? Since I returned from St Lucia, I haven't ridden a mile outdoors. I've been concentrating more on swimming, strength training and the odd indoor cycling class. By the time I ride off into the darkness very early one morning between Christmas and New Year it has been more than four weeks since my last bike ride. Rob has advised me that this time of the week – Sunday morning, seven o'clock, to be exact – provides the perfect opportunity for nervous road bikers like me to get a longish ride under their saddles without having their confidence knocked by fast-moving vehicles. And in one way, he's right – the traffic is virtually non-existent and I make it to Richmond Park from Tooting in around twenty minutes despite maintaining a cautious, stately pace. When I arrive the suggestion of an impending sunrise glints at me from behind the tree-lined horizon. The view in the foreground too is undeniably beautiful – a huge expanse of frost-tipped grass with nothing but an incline here, or the occasional roaming deer there, to break it up.

I breathe in the silence of the park, a place where, like my elder sister and brother before me, I learned to ride a bike, my father lovingly holding the back of my saddle and teaching me how to balance on two wheels. As children, my siblings and I stuck to grassy tracks far away from cars, but as an adult I've ridden the ten-kilometre road route that circumvents the park several times over the years.

Yet today I don't feel as at home here as I'd like. The weather has been brutal of late, lashing windows with serious gales, and now it's around two degrees, with an added wind chill that makes my three layers of clothing feel like little more than a vest top. First I lose the feeling in my toes and next my nerve as I narrowly miss a patch of ice. My brain starts freezing a little too: thoughts come and go slower than normal; it's hard to make any decision, any movement, any sound. I can handle the skinny tyres typical of a road bike, but the combination of these with drop-down handlebars, the feeling of having one's feet clipped into the pedals *and* the potentially slippery roads makes me feel very unsteady indeed. All year round though I see apparently fearless cyclists zipping along. What's their secret? Where do they hide their fear? Or are they just wired up differently from me? Because, I'll admit it, I'm really scared.

What if I fall out here? I could very easily hit a patch of black ice and go down. Sure, I have a bank card in the back pocket of my cycling top, along with some cash, my phone and house keys. But if I'm unconscious, how can I call for help? I've seen just one other cyclist pass so far, now no more than a flashing red light dropping down over a hill some three hundred metres away. I don't even know how to fix a puncture, I remember, feeling angry at myself for never bothering to learn. The thought of getting a flat tyre five kilometres into the park, and having to walk back to the nearest bus stop and wait for an intermittent Sunday bus service to begin, is just too much.

I turn the bike around and head out of the park. I'm relieved at this decision to retreat, but can't help feeling that somehow I've lost the battle again against my ever-increasing fear of cycling. It was the right thing to do though – even the journey home feels torturous, my joints are stiff and my jaw is locked with the cold – and after turning onto my road with its view of familiar terraced cottages, stacked up close to one another like books on a library shelf, I step off the bike and sigh.

It is over. Until the next time, at least. My feet are on flat ground again, I'm a few steps away from a very hot drink and –

Ouch!

I slip on a patch of ice. All that fuss about falling off the bike and it happens now, outside the house, when I'm unclipped and about to step up from the road onto the pavement.

The winter sun shines down on me from an empty, bright blue sky after days of stormy rain. It is one minute past nine on what's probably the quietest Sunday morning of the year and, still holding the bike's crossbar in one hand and my helmet in another, I start to cry.

Maybe it was the cold. The fear. I've been tensing for over an hour, gripping the handlebars, clenching my jaw, stiffening my back, always half ready for a fall. I was so tightly strung, in fact, that I didn't even realise how upset I felt until now. It's more than just the temperature though; somewhere between home and Richmond Park I fell into the horrible, well-worn pattern of giving myself hell:

Should be better.

Should do more.

Not successful enough.

Not strong enough.

Why so timid and so weak?

Why so frightened on the bike?

The thoughts weigh on top of one another, crushing the smaller, fragile ones that whisper positives from underneath: *doesn't matter, life is love, you're healthy, it's enough.*

I call it my pressure cooker – the way all the words and phrases bubble up inside what becomes my very noisy mind. During these periods, which last sometimes hours, sometimes days and sometimes weeks, I bite my nails, listen to too much evocative music on big noise-cancelling headphones, and fight back tears at the most inappropriate moments. I stop doing the things that help me feel balanced, loved and well and instead hammer myself with never-ending goals, demands and work. It's hard to know, often until much later, what has switched my pressure cooker on, and what can help to turn it down a notch. Usually it boils until it spills right over. Tears. Panic. Just like now, my icicle-hands shoved under my armpits and elbows crossed in front of my chest. I want to be somebody who would stay out and do several laps of the park. I want to be somebody who enjoys the adrenalin rush of riding across a city where a driver's failure to look in their blind spot can mean sudden death. I want to be a cyclist, so much, I always have. But I am nothing of the sort. What's more, I feel as if recently training has begun to let me down. Whereas it used to lessen anxiety, it's now become a source of concern itself – one of the biggest anxieties of all.

I should have done more swimming this week, I think to myself. *Should have got out on the bike and faced my fear again*. I think I'm falling behind where I ought to be by now, four months into my triathlon year. I really must make a proper, official training schedule. One that I can stick to instead of chopping and changing to suit my work or social life. But maybe it's all useless anyway. What if my hip doesn't right itself in time for the next triathlon? What if I can't ever run again? It's just five months until the season starts. I should have done more. Nothing is enough. But then again, it never is, never has been.

I thought it might provide the ultimate test of my resolve to maintain perspective but now I'm wondering if it's too much. Perhaps triathlon is actually the worst possible sport for me, or for anybody prone to guilt and self-castigation. Because of its multifarious demands, I'm finding myself even more vulnerable to this kind of negative thinking than ever. Three disciplines to obsess over, to perfect, to spend time and money on. Not just this, in fact, but different disciplines within the disciplines – as pool swims must be balanced with open water and wetsuit practice, and focusing on indoor cycling (useful for building power and endurance) means a loss of road skills. Even with running, there are speed sessions and longer endurance runs to tick off, as well as the brick sessions that every experienced triathlete knows and hates.

Here's an issue triathletes face across the globe: whatever you're doing, you should also be doing something else and something more. Your swimming gets better, but your cycling suffers. Become more confident on the bike? That's brilliant, but the hours it's taken have pulled you away from the pool. Improved your run time? Great. Now you're injured again, so back to swimming. It's a bit like the arcade game we played as kids – Whac-a-mole – where you smash one plastic mole on the head with a mallet only to find another mole pops up, almost immediately, from a different hole. Unless you're a full-time triathlete who can put in two or more sessions, four or five hours, per day (along with the necessary warm-up, stretching, massage and siesta), something, somewhere, has always got to give. You're always playing catch-up. You're never quite prepared. Whac-a-mole here? There's another mole – there, and there, and there and there and there.

No wonder that Bella, who knows and understands me better than anybody else in the world, is worried. With all this propensity for self-hatred, humiliation and fear, and with my history of slipping into periods of depression immediately after traumatic or highly pressurised times of life, should I really be doing this?

The tears continue. I'm inside the house now, sitting on the kitchen table with legs swinging childishly underneath to keep me warm and watching the bike that leans accusingly against the wall. Bella holds me tight, enveloping me in her ridiculous fluffy pink dressing gown, before telling me to go upstairs and rest. She knows that right now there is little she can say, but a few things that she can offer, like love, reassurance and hot chocolate. I lie in bed, taking over twenty minutes to stop shivering, and ask myself a very important question: will I be able to complete my self-assigned year in triathlon without destroying my mental health and wellbeing in the process?

The pressure cooker bubbles . . .

Right now I just don't know.

A couple of days later, one dark evening at the tail end of December, I pick up the phone to forty-three-year-old Glaswegian Jane Egan. We've been put in touch by Paralympian Baroness Tanni Grey-Thompson, whom I met at an event held by the Women's Sport and Fitness Foundation a few weeks ago. I explained to Tanni that I was embarking upon a year in triathlon with the express intention of discovering not just what the sport might offer me, but what it offers all sorts of women, from different walks of life. I had plenty of able-bodied triathletes willing to come forward and share their stories, I said, but I was keen also to find a paratriathlete who might talk to me.

Jane's name quickly came up and a few emails later here we are. I'm a little nervous when she answers, aware from the background reading I've done about Jane that much of our conversation will involve grisly subject matter. I don't wish to add to the weight of her suffering with incessant questioning.

As it turns out, I needn't have worried. It becomes immediately clear that Jane is friendly, communicative and keen to help me if she can. As she begins to talk, I struggle to digest the facts of Jane's journey, how her life has been upended during the last four years. After rupturing her Achilles tendon during a little over-zealous dancing at a party in September 2007, Jane was admitted to hospital for repair surgery. As a high-flying lawyer with a penchant for keeping fit, she was keen to resume her normal routine as soon as possible, so began the rehabilitation process with characteristic rigour. But very quickly it became obvious something was wrong; she wasn't making the progress she or the medical professionals had expected. She had been told to swim, but every time she did, she found she could not kick properly. She had been told it would be painful, but not that she would need to stuff down the maximum dose of over-the-counter painkillers to survive.

Instead of gradually healing from the surgery, Jane found herself beset by a series of strange and unpleasant symptoms. Months passed. The leg on which the operation had been performed was purple from the knee down and freezing. After weeks of back-and-forth between her orthopaedic surgeon and physiotherapist, she was finally referred to a pain-management nurse.

Jane was asked if her pain was a stabbing pain. Yes, it was, she nodded.

She was asked if it was a burning pain. Yes, that too, she said.

The diagnosis slowly, and dreadfully, arrived: this pain was neuropathic. Jane was suffering from Complex Regional Pain Syndrome (CRPS), a relatively rare condition, often resulting from an injury, but which persists long after the injury has healed and leads to severe pain that can worsen, rather than improve, over time. It has left her mostly wheelchair-bound; she can walk a few steps but the movement disorders associated with her essential pain-relieving medication make it difficult to do more.

Initially there was the sheer relief of actually having a diagnosis. Jane had spent months wondering if she was, in fact, just going mad. But quickly the grim reality set in. She was signed off work. Her boyfriend, Mel, was stunned. Together they tried to wrap their minds around this news. CRPS disrupts the signalling between the brain and the spinal cord; it interrupts the peripheral nervous system; it affects blood flow and tissue growth; it affects nail growth and bone density; it affects the ability to build muscle and increases the risk of osteoporosis. Jane began to develop a bizarre movement in her foot over which she had absolutely no control. The pain moved up her leg, into the other leg, and soon she was able to chart its progress around her entire body.

The future was terrifying and uncertain, particularly since, by her own admission, Jane lost all faith in the medical profession. She went to a neurologist, who suggested there was basically nothing to worry about. In the summer of 2008 Jane was sent for various tests to rule out a number of other potential diagnoses, just in case there was something else untoward, worsening things. The other nasties were duly ruled out. But still nobody knew what to do about the CRPS. Best of luck, they said, and that was that. She was referred back to another physiotherapist. Full circle and none the wiser.

By now Jane was living with constant, excruciating pain. (Experts rate CRPS as the most severe pain there is, significantly more severe than that experienced by women during childbirth without anaesthesia, or during the amputation of a digit.) She describes a kind of snapping, electric sensation, as if she had been plugged into the mains. Life looked very, very bleak and Jane's mood had dropped to an all-time low.

But then, in 2009, something momentous happened. Some of Jane's friends had signed up for the Glasgow Half Marathon, and she decided to join them on the start line. Three weeks before the event, Jane spent three days in Cambridge having a race chair designed, made and fitted. She had no idea what she was doing – getting the three wheels of a race chair to move and turn at speed is surprisingly technical, she explains. It requires the use of really small muscles which, if not conditioned, can become exhausted long before the race is run. The day of the half marathon arrived and she had barely had time to practise. Somehow, rather slowly, she made it through. What's more, she enjoyed herself immensely.

Next came a sprint triathlon. Jane had got to grips with the race chair and also purchased a hand bike. She knew she could manage thirty lengths of the pool, despite still having virtually no kick, and before she knew it, she had completed her first triathlon and officially caught the bug.

In 2010, Jane travelled to Loughborough to find out more about her options, what disability classification she might fit into and whether she would ever be allowed to compete. She joined in with those hoping to be chosen for the Great Britain squad.

'I was swimming granny breaststroke with no float,' she says. 'My legs just sank! It was terrible!'

To her shock and delight, Jane discovered that there was nobody in her particular disability category, and she was picked, purely on potential, to represent her country in the sport of paratri. She received a small grant towards the costs of her coaching and that year became Paratri 1 (P1) British, European and World Champion. In 2011 and 2012, she maintained her European Champion status, and in 2011 and 2013 was also crowned World Champion. When we speak in December, her most recent accolade is a win at the ITU World Triathlon Grand Final in September 2013.

It has been a long and moving conversation. After hanging up the phone, I wait a while inside my study to digest what I've heard before rejoining Bella and the television downstairs. I think how, particularly in relation to Jane but also in smaller ways for all of us, triathlon is like a leech. It sucks the blood out of us and leaves its mark, a lovebite, upon our skin. Yet it also enables healing, helping to get the blood pumping around the body. It saps our life force and it enlivens us. Deny this contradiction and you'll get nowhere. Accept it? The world bulges with possibility.

8

With Rob's guidance and instructions, my swimming continues to improve throughout the winter. I've been doing one kilometre minimum at least once a week since I returned from St Lucia. I have no real goal in sight beyond simply building my swimming ability and cardiovascular endurance so that I can do freestyle continuously for the thirty-five or forty minutes I'm guessing it'll take for me to complete the 1500-metre swim in an Olympic-distance triathlon.

The truth is, however, that for the most part I still find it boring. Some people talk about the joy of moving through the water as an end in itself, but I am, quite simply, not one of those people. Nor is cycling going much better, given my recent tearful trip to Richmond Park, and because of my injury I still can't run much either.

'This isn't going to work,' I tell Bella, rather dramatically, one night in late January, around the date generally agreed to be the most depressing of the year. 'It's like being half in love with someone. It's utterly pointless. I'll have to end it. Just end it all.'

It takes a beat or two before she realises that I am not, in fact, talking about our relationship but about the love–hate affair I'm having with triathlon.

'This is supposed to be fun,' she says. 'Just take the pressure off. Remember, this is all your choice. It's something you want to do. I thought the whole point was to try and approach it less intensely than you've approached things like this before. You know, to enjoy the process and all that?'

Ah yes, I remember. At the beginning it wasn't about *should* or *must* or *not enough hours in the day*. It was about learning something new (like swimming), about challenging myself (facing my fears) and uncovering why women love triathlon.

Thanks to my wife's astute reminder, I'm able to take a step back and recalibrate. Serendipitously perhaps, it is after this, with some semblance of perspective regained, that Emily and I start chatting about my training. I need to get things going, I explain, and she suggests that I join her at the training camp this April at Club La Santa in Lanzarote. It has come up in conversation before, but I have pooh-poohed the idea as expensive, difficult and even a little self-indulgent.

This time, however, something has changed and I don't decline immediately.

'You get to live like an athlete,' she says. 'It's ten days of just training, eating and sleeping. Again and again. And then at the end we do the Volcano Tri – Olympic distance only!'

Train, eat and sleep? Over and over again, and nothing more or less than that? It's not the worst idea I've ever heard.

'Can beginners go?' I ask. 'Will I be coached?'

'Yes, absolutely,' she says. 'The camp is split into different groups, sorted by ability.'

Olympic distance . . . At the end of April. Will I – could I – be ready for that? I'm still learning to swim competently, still fairly nervous on the bike, still unable to run at all. It would be foolish to undertake something so huge. Ambitious, arrogant even. But I don't care. I want that Lanzarote Triathlon on my list. I close my eyes, pretend I'm running, comfortably and freely, and I can feel it in my legs. It will happen, I will manage.

I book my flights the next day. Perhaps it's the thought of having ten days abroad in April to fully immerse myself in triathlon, or maybe it's just the slow waning of winter, but by late January things start to shift. One Friday evening I hit the pool for my weekly session, which begins in the usual unpleasant way. Where is the oxygen I need? I try to exhale evenly and to not panic when I turn my head for breath. Beneath me at the bottom of the pool I can see the odd clump of hair, a plaster and . . . is that a trail of blood? I once heard someone say that if God had wanted us to smoke, he'd have equipped us with chimneys on our knees. Well, if God had wanted us to swim, he or she would have given us blowholes instead of knees, and ensured there were plenty of heated open-air pools available to use for free, rather than murky Leisure Centres that threaten verrucas for all who dare to walk barefoot through their halls. But then something quite amazing happens. I realise when I reach the end of the pool for the twenty-ninth time that it's the first time I've *not* wanted to stop. During these last blissful thirty-three metres, I haven't been worrying about my breathing, nor reminding myself how rubbish I am at this sport. I've just been focusing on kicking steadily, with almost straight legs and big toes nearly brushing together (another of Rob's tips, a way of getting the swimmer to use the muscles in their bottom and not displace excess water with vicious knee-bend kicks).

The rest of the swim is the best yet. I calculate, with glee, that I've managed the whole sixty lengths – two kilometres – in around forty-seven minutes, and go to bed that night feeling hopeful and excited.

_◦◦◦_

The following morning I am up early to meet fellow St Lucian triathlete Paula at Richmond Park for a ride. Again, the Tri Gods are smiling on me. It takes just ten minutes to begin feeling comfortable on the road bike, which I haven't used since that horrible icy day a month ago. This time I'm dressed better: two pairs of leggings, two pairs of gloves, two long-sleeved T-shirts underneath my cycle top, a beanie hat under my helmet and a muff around my neck. The temperature, in any case, is warmer, and after a wet start the sun emerges as I arrive at the park.

Today, things just work. I understand why triathletes – and cyclists – so often train in groups; I'm not sure I'd have made it out at all if I didn't have a pre-existing engagement to keep. The pressure is reduced with Paula, too, who's a less experienced athlete and a more relaxed companion than Ren. My hip is feeling all right and, although I've got a twinge in my right foot now, I find myself full of energy and confidence. What's more, it seems natural to be cleated into the pedals. Perhaps my neuromuscular system has finally adapted and become used to clipping in and out in an instant. On the downhill parts I am still scared and feather the brakes continually, terrified of falling and engaged in dramatic imaginings of my bloodied carcass. But on the uphill

I'm getting stronger and I know it; the agony of this winter's weekly indoor cycling classes is beginning to pay off.

We do two laps (around twenty kilometres) before stopping for coffee and cake. I ask Paula about her background, and how and why she first came across triathlon. At school she played team games and then at university she moved on to rowing. Since then, she's used sport as a means of mending a broken heart or elevating a downcast mind. Back in 2010, finding herself between jobs, aged forty and single, she decided to cycle a thousand kilometres from Calais to Chamonix, completely unaided and alone.

'I bought a bike, panniers and a map. I decided against one with contours though, as I didn't want to play mind games with the hills and try easier routes. I went pretty much the next day. And when you look at my route it was virtually a straight line between the two towns. I didn't have a tent or anything – just rocked up in a town and stayed in B & Bs and hotels. I did the thousand kilometres in eleven days with one rest day!'

My eyebrow rises. Paula's gentle demeanour and big laugh are deceptive. That self-effacing smile clearly hides a hard-core nature.

'Actually I ended up in St Lucia largely because of a relationship break-up,' she goes on. 'That was last Easter and . . . well, let's just say, I know if I have too much time on my hands and stew about things I get very down.'

Instead of allowing herself to fall Paula did something proactive and threw herself into sprint-distance triathlons, beginning with the Thames Turbo series held in Hampton, apparently excellent for novices since it involves pool rather than open water swimming. Paula did breaststroke in the swimming part of those races. But by the time she got into the water in St Lucia a few months later she was swimming front crawl all the way.

It's not just triathlon she's set her sights on either. This March, she reveals, she's doing the fifty-four-kilometre Birkebeiner cross-country ski marathon in Norway.

'By the way,' she adds, 'I'm looking into doing several legs of racing in the Clipper Round the World Race in 2015–16.'

I shudder because, *by the way,* being stuck on a boat for weeks, isolated from friends, family and home? It sounds, to me, like total and utter hell.

'Why?' I laugh.

'I always need the next goal. Without it I feel lost and rudderless. It would be nice to do these things with a partner, but hey . . .'

She shrugs and the conversation changes direction, towards which events we're both entering this season. It's usually around now, at the start of a new calendar year, that triathletes begin to chatter about their new goals, and how they'll distribute their money in order to meet them. It can, for the less wealthy, take quite some planning. The average Olympic triathlon costs £60–100 just to take part, before you've invested in gear or paid for transport and accommodation. As for deciding which one to do, it's not just cost that can be influential in making a choice, but also the nature of the event itself. These vary hugely. There are mass events with thousands of competitors like the London Triathlon, held annually around the Docklands, and the New York Triathlon, which has a similarly large field of entrants and is renowned for its super-fast swim due to strong currents in the Hudson river. (It is also famous for the sudden death of both a sixty-four-year-old man and a forty-year-old woman in 2011, said to be the result of cardiac issues during the swim.) The smaller, more niche events, such as 'women only', which is an increasingly popular category are often cheaper and frequently part of a series of three or four spread out over the season, allowing triathletes to monitor their progress more easily as spring goes into summer. Each and every triathlon has its own distinct character, however, its own positives and negatives. Some are very oversubscribed, and others need more support.

In short, there's so much choice, it's mind-blowing.

But it wasn't always this way. There was a time before women like Paula could distract themselves from heartache with a new physical challenge. Before tri-hards like Ren and Emily could set higher goals for themselves each year, looking at life through the Technicolor lens of a recreational athlete. Because there was a time when not everybody knew someone who took part in marathons, triathlons or adventure races. Astoundingly, the first recorded usage of 'triathlon', according to the *Oxford English Dictionary* online, was on 21 July 1973, when the *Daily Telegraph* reported: 'A new event called the "Triathlon". In this all four members of a team have to demonstrate their prowess in clay pigeon shooting, fly fishing and riding a handy hunter-course over jumps.'

Much, I'm sure, to the incredulity of shooting and fishing fans, this particular type of triathlon didn't catch on, though the swim–bike–run kind did in a fairly major way. On 25 September 1974 the first recorded triathlon was hosted on

Mission Beach in California. Some nine years after that, on 5 June 1983, triathlon made its UK debut near Reading. Initially referring purely to an Ironman (or similar) distance, triathlon gradually began to develop shorter forms too – more manageable for non-endurance athletes. Since then, its growth has been extraordinary. At the time of writing, the International Triathlon Union (ITU) says there are a whopping 3.4 million active triathletes globally and over ten thousand events. And since 2007, says Multisport Research, there has been a 111 per cent increase in triathlon participation worldwide.

Picking and choosing which events, distances and locations will suit my aims has not been easy but I'm whittling things down, I explain to Paula. In April I have the tri-training camp, just recently booked, with an Olympic triathlon. Then two sprint events in London and Oxfordshire in the diary for early June, followed by a grand finale at the end of August, in Chantilly in northern France. It is one of a series of Castle Triathlons, famous for stunning locations, welcoming atmospheres and fabulous after-parties.

'Oooooh! I'll do the French one with you,' says Paula.

It'll be her first ever Olympic-distance triathlon.

'Really?'

I'm thrilled. The more I get to know Paula, the more I admire, like and respect her. I'd love to stand shoulder to shoulder with her before diving into an Olympic tri together.

We spin through a few more topics – men we've dated, psychotherapy, Paula's potential move up to Scotland – before saying our goodbyes. I cycle home feeling humbled and inspired.

As soon as I get home I send a message to Ren to spread the good news: *Had a bit of a breakthrough in the pool yesterday! Then two laps of Richmond Park this morning.*

Only two laps? she replies.

Um, yeah, but I felt good on the bike for the first time, so that's a big deal, right?

Did you time your laps? asks Ren.

No! It was a social ride, I explain.

Next time, time your laps, is the response. *It's always good to time laps as a benchmark.*

OK, I reply. *It was just so good to feel confident though. That's the main thing, right?*

Great. So next time we ride, we can put the hammer down. Next weekend, London to Windsor and back?

With trepidation I agree.

In the event, the weather is so atrocious – storms have been thrashing Britain's south-west coast for days and even inland – that parts of the London-to-Windsor cycle route are completely waterlogged and it becomes clear we must postpone.

'Don't worry,' says Ren. 'You can come and turbo instead.'

I hesitate. 'Turbo?'

The noun refers to a turbo trainer, a bilateral frame that attaches to the back wheel of your bike. The average cost of a half-decent one is £300, but the freedom it affords is arguably well worth it; the turbo trainer allows you to practise indoors, on your own bike, and this, according to Rob, can have astoundingly positive results on bike-handling skills when people re-enter the road environment. It enables them to become not just a whole lot fitter, but also more consciously competent on the bike when weather or time doesn't allow for long outdoor rides. It also means that any cyclist can do the type of training that's best for him or her, rather than adopt a kind of fitness utilitarianism – doing what's best for an entire class full of people at varying levels of skill and fitness.

Ren insists the turbo trainer really comes into its own in training to maintain power over a long(ish) duration. That's where the verb comes in. *To turbo.* It means to commit. It means to push. It means to hurt.

'The girls from the tri club used to come over on Sunday morning sometimes,' Ren tells me. 'I'd push all the furniture back and they'd bring their turbos and we'd all turbo together. It was hell,' she adds, as if this will encourage me. 'But I'll do my turbo session before you arrive so I can be all relaxed to watch you suffer!'

I step across the threshold of Ren's pristine west London abode at nine thirty that Sunday morning. The first thing I notice upon entering is that everything, repeat *everything*, has its place, the decor is perfect, the carpet unmarked, the furniture barely showing signs of human use. But slap bang in the middle of the living room, Ren's road bike sits atop the triangular contraption I've heard so much about.

There's a fresh sweat towel and two full water bottles on the bike. Ren has been waiting for me, clearly. And, as promised, she has already done her training for the day.

In an obvious ploy to defer activity for another five minutes, I tell Ren about Emily and the triathlon training camp I've booked in Lanzarote in just two and a half months' time.

'Camps are great for making huge improvements in a really short space of time,' she says. 'That'll be really, really useful. And the tri at the end of it will be a bonus. What's Emily's surname?'

She starts pressing buttons on her phone. I know exactly what's going on. Ren is checking online for Emily's results in any major races, probably interested in where she stands in comparison to Emily, and, I fear, where Emily stands in comparison to me.

Is this tendency to contextualise one's ability a feature unique to triathlon or just Ren's mindset? I fear it's both but I'm beginning to suspect that the age-group categories in triathlon allow it to become fiercely competitive even when done on a purely recreational level. Thus rendering it slightly less 'recreational' after all . . .

We turn our minds back to Ren's bike, as I step, literally, into Ren's shoes and clip into the pedals.

'Is this a bit like spinning?' I ask.

Ren shoots me a sly grin I've come to know and hate. Something tells me this is going to be *nothing* like spinning.

'So warm up for five minutes,' she says. 'And then do this.'

She thrusts a folded white piece of paper marked 'Turbo set for Lucy' into my left hand, which, after three minutes at an easy pace, already feels a bit clammy. The 'set' consists of intervals and requires me to maintain, on several occasions, *90 rpm*. Of course I've seen this magic number – ninety revolutions per minute – in Ren's email to me, sent on the eve of Tri St Lucia. It's more familiar now – I know that it's often regarded as the most energy-efficient number of pedal turns for those wishing to cover any kind of distance at speed. Hold this cadence (the generic term for any given rpm) by using the gears, so when you hit a hill you can drop the gear down and keep those legs whizzing around at the same speed.

But there's also another number that's important in Ren's plan. It refers to wattage, the official term for power output, and Ren wants me to keep mine between 175 and 210 for the majority of the session. There is, of course, a small gadget on her bike that measures this wattage, along with various other bits of data like distance, speed and the all-important revolutions per minute too.

It is a long set for my first time on the turbo, where the pace is generally far tougher than riding out on city roads, because (sadly) there's no need to stop. From the outset it feels as though my bike is dragging against something – as if I'm cycling through mud or on unsmooth terrain. I am to start with four sets of five minutes, holding that 175 wattage, with a minute's easy riding recovery in between. Then I'll switch to four sets of four minutes with a forty-five-second recovery between each, and then to four sets of three with a thirty-second recovery.

Ren slumps down noisily on the sofa.

'Oh, I'm going to take a little seat and relax with this coffee while you *work*!'

'This is hard,' I whimper, shamefully.

'*This* is base training,' Ren says.

I don't need to ask what it means. I might not know the exact science, but I know what she is really saying: this has to be the worst of my best; it only gets tougher from here.

Instinctively, when I'm really tiring, I sit up, taking my hands off the handlebars.

'Get your freaking hands back on those hoods!' she barks.

She's right of course. On the road or in a race environment my hands can only move from 'the hoods' – or tops of the handlebars – if they are going down to 'the drops'. I won't be able to just sit up and take a breather; I've got to learn. But this is definitely a whole new level of nasty. My legs feel at points like something (lactic acid? Blood?) might actually erupt out of them, bursting through the skin and spraying all over Ren's pristine living room. I want it to end, so much, but we are still only halfway through. Thinking about the future of the workout is disastrous, I discover. You must think just of now, and not expect that it will hurt this much for the entire thing. Otherwise you simply won't finish.

It must be clear that I'm struggling now. So Ren reveals her trump card:

'You're going to need to work on your relationship with pain,' she says with the eye-glint of an evil temptress, 'if you want to beat Emily in that triathlon . . .'

She knows me too damned well already.

'What are her times like then?' I ask, trying to appear nonchalant.

'I reckon you could beat her,' says Ren, looking at her phone's screen. 'Maybe not this season, but next. If you stop arsing around in your training. But you're gonna try and beat her in Lanzarote, right?'

I take the cadence up a notch. I'm following the plan that sits atop my handlebars, now blotted with sweat: 210 watts for two minutes. I can't speak until it's done and there's a minute of 'riding easy'.

'When did you actually start triathlon?' I ask.

'2007,' she says. 'What were you doing in 2007, Fry?'

I laugh, the extra movement displacing yet more sweat from my face and onto the handlebars. There are so many answers I could give: working in publishing, overspending, grappling with my sexuality, drinking too much . . . But I think I know what she means.

'The New York Marathon,' I say.

Her ears prick up. 'Oh really? What time did you do it in?'

My head drops. 'Five and a half hours,' I manage, though it's becoming harder and harder to speak.

Clearly, Ren finds this hysterical. 'Were you wearing a weighted vest at the time?'

'Touché,' I say, relieved to be entering another one minute of recovery riding. 'Actually I was ill – some gastric bug. But also I had no idea what I was doing. I didn't train properly back then. I didn't eat the right things either. I was a mess!'

'Oh God, me too,' she replies.

Ren describes her first triathlon – the London Triathlon – and how she knew nothing about interval training or weekly and monthly training structures. I'm reminded of Suzanne, and Emily too, come to think of it – for all of them the first event involved less than perfect preparation. Ren, perhaps unsurprisingly, took things to extremes. She sat on the rowing machine for forty-five minutes to increase general cardiovascular fitness and leg strength, or went to spin classes instead of biking outdoors. Then she bought a wetsuit on the internet that didn't fit, for £50, and so tight was it across the shoulders that she found herself walking to the start line of her first triathlon like the Michelin Man.

Ren still finished her first Olympic-distance triathlon in well under three hours. And when her brother suggested they try a longer distance together, she took the plunge and signed up for the Wimbleball Half Ironman, known, due to its difficulty, as the 'Three-quarter Ironman', in 2010. This time she included interval training, turbo training and proper swim training in her schedule. Like Suzanne, she had a demanding full-time job but often trained twice a day during the week and woke up around five or six in the morning on weekends so as to get a four- or five-hour cycle ride in before lunch.

Five hours every weekend? It's hard to imagine having that kind of relentless commitment and drive. I've been on this turbo trainer for about forty-five minutes and I'm already completely spent.

Ren finished Wimbleball in an impressive six hours and fifteen minutes. Next she set her sights on qualifying for the Half Ironman World Championships (for non-elite racers) in Las Vegas. The actual event, she tells me, was 'awful'. It was forty degrees and she was, understandably, severely overheated and dehydrated by the end. No matter. Afterwards she went out drinking with some friends and got to bed at 2 a.m.

But, hangovers aside, Ren hadn't finished with long-distance triathlon. In 2012, she decided, it was time to go the whole hog.

'I liked the rush of Half Ironman training, so I said to myself, right, let's do an Ironman next year. So I did an Ironman the following year. But actually, training for a full Ironman was a bit disappointing, because it wasn't very intense. It was just very . . . long. So I kind of felt a bit cheated, training my fucking tits off for twenty-five hours a week and . . .'

Ren never finishes her sentence and I'm too tired to press her to. Instead I drop the gears down and breathe deeply for several seconds. It is my final minute of easy riding before starting my last three-minute set of hard, hard work.

I need a story to get me through it.

'The toughest?' I ask, breathlessly. 'What's been the worst, y'know . . . uh . . . like . . .'

It's all I can manage. I can't talk and keep the cadence and power up at the same time. But Ren has the answer already, anyway: Ötillö.

Ah yes. The SwimRun championship that she and her friend Penny completed as a team last summer and which Suzanne and Emily have set their sights on this year, 2014. We've discussed it before, but only in passing. I've never really heard the details, the time hasn't been right. But now I want to know.

'I went to some dark places there.' She breathes. 'You're so fucked, it's just . . .' Pause. 'Penny had to pull me out and say stop having negative thoughts. I was feeling so sick, my shoulders felt like I was being beaten with sledgehammers. Penny told me negative thoughts increase your heart rate by two beats a minute . . . she kept saying just get to that next marker – the next hundred metres or something – it's all about tiny goals, tiny goals, and that's very hard to do when you're that beaten up. But the thing is, for Ötillö I didn't train hard enough . . . I completely underestimated what I had to do – if it hadn't been for Penny, and my pride, I wouldn't have got round. But also, had I stopped, she wouldn't have been able to finish [the rules of Ötillö state it is a paired event], but literally every step I was just breaking down further and further, thinking when is this going to end. And as for the chafing!'

You have to run in your wetsuit and swim either wearing your running shoes or with them in a waterproof bag in between your legs. That alone might be enough to tip me over the edge, I think. How does Ren – and how will Suzanne and Emily – do it? And why? There must be gold at the end of the rainbow, I guess. Just like in St Lucia, only greater.

'In the last few swims . . .' she continues, 'urgh, they're only short swims but you have no power left. The swims for Ötillö, you've gotta go in at an angle because of the current and if you get that wrong . . . I missed it and there was a current coming into me and waves and being bashed against rocks and so I literally managed to grab a rock and pull myself in. They were watching like – if you need help, OK, but you're disqualified. But you can't really train for that in the UK – there's nowhere like the Stockholm archipelago.'

Dark places. Hadn't trained hard enough. Bashed against the rocks . . . None of it stopped her, two weeks later, competing for Ireland as an age-group athlete in the World Championships in Hyde Park, where, with inclement weather necessitating that competitors did a 750-metre swim rather than 1500 metres, Ren finished in two hours eighteen minutes. Two weeks after that, she tells me, Ren completed the Aix-en-Provence Half Ironman. Her finishing time was five hours, fifty-five minutes and fourteen seconds.

I sit back a moment. Two minutes of easy riding to cool down. About an hour of turboing almost over. It's one of the most intense workouts I've done for a while. I mop up the sweat from the creases in my face and off the crossbar of the bike and unclip the pedals so I can step off, thigh muscles twitching, every part of my clothing sodden with sweat.

'So what's next?' I ask once I've recovered a little breath.

'Well, my happy place is in a gym,' says Ren. 'I love lifting weights. Love being strong. I want to enjoy the social side of triathlon and training a bit more. To go there, do a race, have a good craic, go on the town afterwards and not feel guilty about it.'

I nod. Sounds good.

'But . . .' She looks at the wall for a moment. 'Then again, I'd like to do the Norseman one day.'

I gulp. The Norseman, held annually in Norway, claims to be the daddy of all long-distance races. It's known for being hard, wet, cold and lonely. The male-to-female ratio of participants is 85:15. Some people say it's the toughest Ironman-distance event out there but because it's not an Ironman-branded event, it'll never gain the status of toughest Ironman (a title fought over by Ironman Wales, Lanzarote and Hawaii). I feel a little melancholic just thinking about it but I know, for somebody like Ren, the infamous brutality of this race will only make it more attractive.

Could I do the Norseman one day? Probably, as Ren suggests: if I trained accordingly and believed enough that I could do it. Can and will Ren do it? Surely, yes: if this woman wants to achieve something then she will.

'Why do you want to keep doing these long events?' I ask, still busy wiping the sweat away. 'What about sprint or Olympic? Don't they hold any appeal these days?'

'Everybody does sprint distance,' says Ren. 'Everybody does Olympic too these days. But long distances? That's about separating yourself from the ordinary.'

I go quiet awhile and consider this.

'You should do a Half Ironman,' says Ren. 'By the end of this season? You totally could.'

This notion of what constitutes ordinary is on my mind all the way home. Is it wrong that I have no real desire to do the 1900-metre swim, 90-kilometre cycle and 21.1-kilometre run required in a Half Ironman? But are my Olympic-distance aspirations just 'ordinary' too, as Ren suggests? I recall how ex-triathlete Sarah Springman (now heavily involved in the governance of triathlon) once told me that people who do triathlon want to 'live the dream. They know they can't be a Stanford or a Brownlee or a Stimpson or a Jenkins, but they still want the world to know they're something special.'

Do we – do I – want the world to know I'm something special? Probably – we may know it's futile but deep down, don't most of us? But while I may have done other things in life with the misguided belief that they might mark me out in some way, I can put my hand on any holy book and swear that I never entered triathlon with that intention. And anyway, Ren's right – it does feel like a sprint or Olympic-distance triathlon is around every corner nowadays and what makes triathletes special is the longer-distance stuff. Perhaps that's just the nature of sport – we will always find markers to differentiate one person from another – but when it comes to triathlon I am increasingly beginning to suspect there's an issue of double standards.

On the one hand the message is that this is an inclusive and non-judgemental sport where everybody is hailed a triathlete after completing just one event. Hurrah. Well done you. Slap on the back. You're in the club and the standard for entry is participation and nothing more. On the other hand it has become increasingly clear through chatting to Suzanne, Emily and Ren that there is kudos in suffering. The more extreme the suffering, the more kudos. That whole thing about being a part of the gang just for taking part? That's not really true. You're not a real triathlete, not in the *real* club until you've done an Ironman or, at the very least, made it round a tough Half Ironman course. That's where your mettle is truly tested. It's all about long distance and endurance. The further you can take your love of triathlon, the more extraordinary you are. So maybe if you don't take it all the way, right down to the end of the road, you don't actually love it at all?

In the short time it takes to drive my scooter back south of the river I think seriously about changing my plan in a bid to uncover the supposed extraordinary triathlete within me. I could include a Half Ironman, as Ren suggested, around mid September. Perhaps that ought to be the pinnacle of my season rather than an 'ordinary' Olympic distance?

But no – this isn't what my Commitment Aide was meant to do! She's taking me away from the plan and off into another dimension. Apart from my existing injury (I nearly forgot) and my Tri Guide's almost certain disapproval (too much, too soon, he'd say) there's also the Relationship Crisis Barometer, which on a couple of occasions recently has just tapped out of the *all fine* zone and into *warning*.

In a bid to stop myself from deviating from my plan or becoming distracted by grandiose goals, I spend the rest of February consolidating. I go over to Ren's once more for a similar turbo torture session the following Sunday. It certainly doesn't look as if spring is coming early this year and I do want the occasional Sunday morning in bed, so I start thinking about buying my own turbo. The cheaper ones look dreadful quality and the reviews online are awful. Really, you're looking at £300 minimum for a turbo that won't destroy your floor, your bike or both. Luckily, Emily kindly offers to lend me hers; she won't need it, she says, not until Ironman training begins in late summer, as she has an issue with her sciatic nerve and is focusing more on swimming at the moment.

I add a weekly turbo threshold session (read: holding a very painful pace for forty minutes or more) to the mix. I'm still not allowed to run, but at least this intense cycling should help me maintain my cardiovascular fitness levels enough that when I do lace up my shoes again I won't be a total mess. I try to get into the red zone a little more with swimming too, adding interval sets into my sessions. Four lengths medium pace. Two lengths easy. Two lengths medium to hard pace. One length easy. One length as fast as possible. One length easy. Repeat. Then go for a burger with the wife. I can't deny myself much on the food front these days; my body tells me what it needs. Letting myself go hungry jeopardises both my mood and the next training session. The most important thing is maintaining energy levels so that I can perform as well as possible week in, week out. Mostly I try to focus on drenching my body in nutrients, filling my plate with a mix of high-quality protein, complex carbohydrates and lots of green cruciferous vegetables. But honestly, if an extra chocolate bar goes in here and a pizza goes down there, so be it. It's still the off season, after all.

9

March – pre-season – arrives and it is time to meet paratri-athlete Jane Egan in person.

As she pulls up outside Glasgow airport to collect me in her car, I see no evidence of her condition. What the typical paratriathlon champion looks like, I obviously have no idea . . . but Egan's tiny frame still takes me by surprise. She's thin, in her forties, with slightly sunken cheeks and half-closed eyes that only seem to widen fully when she smiles.

She leans over and opens the passenger door. I hop in, reminding myself that I'm sitting next to the three-time British, European and World Paratriathlon Champion and, quite possibly, a woman who will bring home a medal for Great Britain in the next Paralympics.

'What's on the agenda for today, then?' I ask, once we've properly greeted one another.

'Not much training, I'm afraid,' she says. 'I'm not feeling so great today, and I'm injured now too.'

I nod, a little disappointed, having hoped to see Jane in action on her hand bike. But I always knew it could be this way, that Jane's condition can throw her schedule complete-ly out of whack and force her to rest instead.

We head to Jane's local health club to sit in the cafe and talk. Three hours pass as we chatter, interrupted only by her friends who stop to say hello, or others who, spotting Jane's

GB paratriathlon top, are curious to know more about her and her sport. They cannot resist asking questions.

'Is that you? Jane?' says one woman. Her words are trimmed with politeness and I notice Jane's demeanour change from interested (in what she's been saying) to re-hearsed (she's told this story, succinctly, many times before); from natural to ever so slightly brittle, almost imperceptibly, just around the edges.

It turns out that she and this lady were colleagues many years ago when Jane was a lawyer, before the onset of her condition forced her to stop work. The older woman is cu-rious, clearly perturbed, and wants to know how Jane has ended up in this wheelchair. Jane's answer is basic but in-formative.

'I had an accident. There were complications. It's a neu-rological thing.'

And that's about it. I'm guessing she has found a way of explaining things to suit her and whomever she's talking to. I'm guessing it must be both unbearable and comforting when people actually stop to ask what's wrong, to acknowl-edge the enormous change they see in Jane. But I'm also guessing that nobody – and nothing – can take away from the sense of powerlessness and frustration that Jane must feel, day in, day out.

When the woman leaves, I ask Jane what she's feeling, right now, as we sit with our drinks, the sound of squash balls clocking against nearby court walls.

'I can feel pain from my knees all the way down to my toes,' she tells me, almost conspiratorially. 'Right now, it's like somebody is crushing both my ankles. And it's funny, you know, actually, because I think you do get a bit better at blocking it out of your consciousness. I think a lot of people fall down at the beginning because they don't understand that they're going to need to learn how to live with the pain . . . I think I went into the whole thing with a fairly realistic expectation. And yes, I've had to try different medications to find the ones that take enough of the pain away with side effects that I can manage to cope with, and have a quality of life that is all right. Yes, I'd like to have a quality of life without these side effects, but I don't think the extra pain would be better for me to try and live with.'

The pain itself also doesn't remain at the same level every day. Instead it cycles up and down, sometimes spiking to an unbearable height, and sometimes returning to a lower, more diffuse level, coursing its way around the body. The medication Jane's now on helps to make these shifts more predictable, with a three-day pain patch cycle. On the first day she'll usually feel fairly good, she tells me, and so she'll try and fit in two training sessions, interspersed with a nap. By the third day, she can often hardly get out of bed.

Today is the third day.

'You've been lucky,' is all she says, and a respectful silence falls between us.

We are none of us immune to neurological pain. An accident or injury, followed by an operation and complicated side effects? Life would never go back to its previous mould. Living with a pain worse than that experienced during childbirth? I feel sick just at the thought. How does Jane cope?

'You're sitting in a wheelchair, catch sight of yourself in a shop window and do a double take because you don't recognise yourself in that form. There's a collective norm around being with people in the same boat – like in paratri – and it makes you feel part of something. It eases the passage through the difficulty.'

But if Jane had wanted to enjoy a little paratri here and there, without allowing it to subsume her life, she would have faced some problems. Competing at a recreational level in paratriathlon wasn't really ever a viable option for her, she explains, because of the logistical complexities surrounding the sport. There are so many factors to consider. Firstly, Jane has far more kit than an able-bodied triathlete. I thought a regular triathlon race involved an inordinate amount of gear but for paratriathletes the stress is doubled – tripled even. What with her wheelchair, her hand bike, her race chair and other necessities, Jane can neither travel to a race, nor move through airports, nor get herself sorted in transition areas, without help. Able-bodied triathletes like me think nothing of an off-road section between transition and the bike course. But for a paratriathlete this is impossible; the hand bike and race chair are both heavy and can't be carried over gnarly tracks where rocks and stones get in the way. Speed bumps in the road are a problem too, Jane explains to me. And it has to be easy to get up and out of the water.

I think back to the course in St Lucia. The beach run from the ocean to transition might have been carpeted over with matting, perhaps. But the bike course, up steep hills, the occasional surprise pothole, not to mention kamikaze drivers on the road? No paratriathlete could have navigated that. I feel a sharp regret at the way I've complained my way through this winter's training. I've whined about the cold and I've bitched about the rain. I've bemoaned the cost involved in triathlon, both physical and financial. But, beyond genuine financial constraints, there has been a certain sense of entitlement, an unappreciated ease with which I have researched various events and begun to cherry-pick the ones that suit my plan. Not to mention taking my body's capabilities for granted (hip injury aside).

I know of course that Jane doesn't want or need my pity – she already has my admiration and respect – what she requires is greater awareness around her condition. In this country, Jane tells me, she has never seen a doctor who knew more about her condition than she did. She has instead been patronised and ignored by supposed experts in their field. She has felt dumped by the system, and has had her subjective reality questioned, as well as her mental health. There has been just one person who captured her attention, and gave her hope, a man resident in the Netherlands who was doing a PhD on her condition back then. He made time and space to see her. She flew over. At last somebody cared enough to research. Somebody listened, really listened, to her. But ultimately, a life without pain is not available to her. Not yet, at least. It was an important and emotional meeting, but there remains little she can actually change.

Today Jane has a physiotherapy appointment, which she and her coach agree I can sit in on. Here a full hour is spent discussing what the best treatment and course of action is for Jane's sore elbow, whose tendon is inflamed, making it difficult for her to use her hand bike for more than fifteen minutes at a time. She must train, she insists, much like any other athlete would: there are various events coming up which are not only important in and of themselves but also because, one by one, each helps her prepare for next year's Paralympic Games qualifiers.

I see in her eyes and hear in her voice just how important this is, how vital a part of her survival; without this purpose and focus, perhaps, she might have given up on real life some time ago. It is maybe more a mere fact than a consolation that without her condition Jane might not have become immersed in a new sport at its exciting, developmental stages. She might never have completed a triathlon, and she would almost certainly never have become an elite athlete and gone on to win gold medals for Great Britain. Being selected on potential, the way she was, simply wouldn't have happened to an able-bodied age-group athlete like Ren or Suzanne or Emily.

On the flight home from Glasgow that evening, my mind is fixed on Jane and the pain that inhabits her life almost every single second, whether awake or asleep, whether training or resting. This may well go on until she dies. She is absolutely clear that she has let go of any ideas of entering remission or being cured, because such a tiny possibility would not in fact give her hope but would bring her further down into despair, anger and a sense of injustice about her situation. But this is not the same as giving up on living, she has insisted many times. In the short time we have spent together it has become clear that the only lining – more scratchy than silver – to this dark cloud is sport. Paratriathlon gives Jane a reason to strive. It offers memorable experiences and the chance to build relationships with other inspirational people. But, over and over again, Jane has made it clear that she would shelve it all for a chance of returning to her old life.

I am inspired by my new friend yet horrified by her pain. I close my eyes for a moment, somewhere, at a guess, many thousands of feet above Yorkshire.

Plugged into the mains.

It is a description I'll never forget.

The day spent with Jane in Glasgow has given me an unexpected jolt and with the training camp looming in little more than a month, I decide it's time to try running again. Since the half marathon last September I've run exactly three times: one twenty-minute jog around my local common where I realised that, yes, I was definitely injured; one five-kilometre 'fun run' in St Lucia the day after arriving; and then the five-kilometre run at the end of the triathlon itself.

Finally, here I am, lacing up my running shoes, ready to go out into the drizzly day, with no sign yet of the much-promised onset of spring.

'Try and stay relaxed,' I tell myself. 'If you tense up, then your hip will know.'

For the first few minutes I'm waiting for something to clonk or clunk or snap. I feel a strong sense of disbelief that I'm actually outside running without that elastic-band feeling in my left leg. My physiotherapist has warned me not to go too far or too fast; he says my sacroiliac joint and the facet joints around the lumbar spine could lock very easily, given too much impact.

I make it round my local common. All in all I'm only running for about twenty-five minutes. Straight afterwards I am feeling good. But a few hours later, it's definitely sore. The next week I go for thirty minutes and I feel even better when I return. But a few hours later, I am in pain again. Feel better, feel worse. That is just how it goes, but these days I've also lost running fitness. I had forgotten the effort – the mental strength (and gameplay) – it takes just to keep going.

'Little and often and you'll get there,' says my physiotherapist. 'Practise running with good form [i.e. spine in alignment, belly tucked in a little and not hunched forward] for just five minutes a day, and build it up from there. Just don't overdo it, right?'

Five minutes a day? Don't overdo it? Does he not understand triathlon?

The slow progress frustrates me on a good day and drives me bonkers on a bad one. Any ideas I had about storming through my first Olympic triathlon are well and truly placed on the back burner. It would be easy to get despondent. Defeatist, even. But I'm hardly the first nor will I be the last triathlete to experience the frustration of injury. Chronically tight hip flexors and rounded shoulders are, I'm told, typical side effects of triathlon, and there are plenty of others for whom the battle against biomechanical issues and injury has been far harder. GB triathlete Helen Jenkins is one example. Her fifth-place finish at the Olympics in 2012 was an extraordinary achievement in itself, but seemed far greater when I learned she couldn't run for ten minutes the day before, and had to have suppository painkillers in order to race at all.

In *220 Triathlon* magazine, Jenkins told Tim Heming: 'The pain was in the knee, but the root cause was at the base of the spine, a slight scoliosis and bulging disc . . . I'd have an injection, a few days off, train for two weeks to see how it felt then have another jab . . . There was a really small bulge at the join of vertebrae L4–L5 and the surgeon used two needles in a scouring action. When he pulled them out it created a vacuum that shrunk the disc by a small amount. It's weird. When so much pain is in your knee, you don't think it's coming from your back. My right glute must have switched off at some point, too. It was noticeable that as soon as I had the procedure it started firing again. It was as if my body had finally clicked back into place.'

Damn those glutes! Weak butt muscles are something Helen and I unwillingly share. Regardless of our varying talents and the differing stakes, we also share ambition, passion and the desire to succeed. By now I'm fairly confident that I can splash my way through 1500 metres in around thirty-two minutes. I need to practise more outdoors on the bike, but I'll definitely be doing that in Lanzarote. The run, in the past the only one of the three triathlon distances that I could say with any surety that I'd manage, is the biggest and mightiest cause for concern. I'm not sure triathlon is good for me, physically, just as I'd be willing to wager that it is no longer physically beneficial for Helen Jenkins's body either. But sometimes larger forces are at work, and things become personal, emotional or spiritual.

However great the sense of purpose, though, there are days when triathlon seems to hold very little reward, nothing I do feels enough and the Whac-a-mole phenomenon is in full force. It's also when my mental pressure cooker starts to bubble, bubble, bubble – when a burgeoning workload necessitates a missed run, or a family Sunday lunch spills over into late afternoon and it's impossible to remember why I had thought that evening swim (after a roast dinner and dessert) was a good idea.

Thanks to Rob's guidance, these missed sessions aren't a big deal. I know that undertraining is less problematic than overtraining, but still . . . For someone with an intrinsic failure complex the essentially unfeasible demands of a perfect week's triathlon training are just a way of feeding a grisly, hairy demon.

Didn't she just go for a twelve-mile run yesterday? I'll think, as Suzanne relates her two-kilometre morning swim yet again. Or – *doesn't she need a day's rest? Should I feel guilty for sometimes taking two per week?* Social media is a killer. One day in late March I read on Emily's Facebook page that she has completed a spin session, a swim, an hour's run and a twelve-kilometre ride, apparently into a headwind, all in one day. When I dare to add a comment that perhaps she's overtraining, Emily quickly responds:

'Lucy, the definition of overtraining is when people train over their capacity without giving their body enough time to recover. This is pretty much a regular day for me, who has a nap in the afternoon and goes to bed at 9.30 p.m., so that's far from overtraining really.'

Actually, the definition of overtraining is far more extensive than that, and recovery isn't just about sleep but also nutrition, hydration, supplementation and lifestyle factors, some of which can vary from person to person. We can normalise anything, even an excessive exercise schedule, but that doesn't mean it's necessarily useful, productive or healthy. The way that Suzanne, Emily and Ren, like many other female triathletes, train – eight to eleven hard sessions a week – can lead to Overtraining Syndrome, particularly when aiming for the longer Olympic, Half Ironman and Ironman events. A slippery little bugger whose symptoms are remarkably similar to depression, Overtraining Syndrome is hard to diagnose and describe. Signs you might be suffering from it include insomnia, low mood, loss or increase of appetite and, rather cruelly, a massive drop in performance. Placing such a heavy training load on one's body, week after week, month after month, can upset the endocrine balance and raise stress hormones, in particular, way beyond a safe level, leading to conditions such as fibro-myalgia and chronic fatigue.

It's often addiction, as much as ambition, that drives us to ignore the body's not-so-subtle signs (pain, exhaustion, illness) that enough's enough. 'We're a sport where you have to have addictive tendencies,' ex-GB triathlete Sarah Spring-man told me once. 'Each year [during the 1980s and 90s, when competing at an elite level], I would get skinnier and skinnier and skinnier, so that in the winter I'd be seventy-four kilos and in summer seventy-two or less [at six foot tall]. Whenever I got to seventy-two kilos, I would be oligo-menorrheic [have infrequent periods].'

Ah yes – weight, fat and performance, a common breed-ing ground for illness and mental health issues. In 2012, the media reported that triathlete Hollie Avil, who represented Team GB in the 2008 Beijing Olympics, had retired from the sport after battling an eating disorder she says was triggered by a comment from another competitor's coach about her being 'a bit heavy' in 2006. Her friend and fellow triathlete Jodie Swallow has also spoken out on her blog about reaching performance weight, as well as her related bulimia and depression.

It's not just professionals, of course, for whom the perceived pressures to look a certain way, and be a certain weight, can take them to breaking point. One of my oldest friends, former amateur triathlete Olivia, found herself in a similarly self-defeating cycle, which placed her health in serious danger, as she tells me in an email:

I was living two lives. I loved the social side of triathlon. What could be better than going for a run, a swim or a cycle, all with friends? But I was also becoming increasingly ill – making myself sick anywhere between one and fifteen times a day, training on top, and my periods had stopped.

The enslavement of it brings a lump to my throat. I share my own experience with Olivia and tell her about the mixed messages I'm getting from triathletes – about how it's all right, on the one hand, just to participate but how, on the other, you have to go further and further to gain respect. Bella is a little worried that I'll be overtaken by the tide, I explain. That I'll push myself too far and stop enjoying it all or even become ill.

Olivia's response is brave and to the point:

I think Bella is right to be a little wary. But I can only tell you what I experienced. The world of triathlon engulfed me as it engulfed many. I saw girls who were struggling and tried to believe that I wasn't like them. I saw men who were obsessed with their physique and their stamina. Rumours of eating disorders amongst amateur and professional athletes were rife; obsessional athletes were commonplace; and training was not just a way of life but it determined life. When one race was done you'd book another one to keep up the momentum. Guilt, anxiety and pressure, all self-inflicted, were daily emotions. A missed training session would bring on a desire to train harder, push harder, work harder and, of course, eat less.

I always suffered from bulimia but when triathlon came along it exaggerated my tendencies tenfold and I found myself in trouble. I am certain I was not alone. I feel a deep sadness when I think about girls, boys, men and women who are struggling alone in the world of triathlon. It's a dark place when it's not going well.

Olivia cut triathlon out of her life, sought professional help for her eating disorder, and began a slow process of recovery:

As far as my bulimia goes, it has affected me, but I feel my body has mostly recovered. I no longer have hard lumps on my hands and fingers or rock-solid lumps in my neck. My eyes are rarely swollen and my digestive system seems to be working well. I have a menstrual cycle, not a regular one but a cycle nonetheless, and it would appear that my physical self is well. I do not know what long-term damage I have done to my stomach and laxative abuse has almost certainly affected my digestive system but not, it would seem, too badly. I've been very lucky indeed. From the age of thirteen to thirty-three I was abusing my body regularly and at thirty-nine I seem to be doing OK. I hope this is true on the inside, as much as I feel it to be true on the outside.

After a while, Olivia returned to swimming, a sport she had always loved. The low-impact, invigorating nature of open water training in particular was a good accompaniment to her recovery, which required less self-punishing activity and a generally slower pace of life.

There are others, however, for whom quite the opposite is true. I discover this after a chance encounter during a three-day course in central London. On the first day I happen to sit next to a young woman who, although I don't know it at the time, has used triathlon to help her overcome an eating disorder. During the course introduction I am distracted by the Ironman rucksack she hugs in between her legs. Jodie, according to her name badge, seems uninterested in what the speaker at the front of the room is saying. I bet she's thinking how much she'd rather be training now. Or about the further training sessions she'll miss because of this course. She looks pretty tired. But since when has that ever stopped a triathlete?

She could, of course, be borrowing this rucksack from a friend or sibling. But something about her muscular legs and the expression on her face tells me otherwise. Besides, I know the (albeit unwritten) rules by now: you don't deign to even touch an Ironman rucksack unless you've completed a race of the same name. I had hoped that on this course I might have a total break from triathlon and yet this tenacious sport doesn't just play on my mind but sits down next to me. It's possible that the owner of this branded bag also fancies a mental respite from her endeavours and I should leave her in peace. But then again . . . Why bring the bag if you're not itching to be asked that crucial question: *did you really do an Ironman?*

It takes me two more days but eventually I make contact. Having seen them hanging around outside together during breaks I've established that Jodie's mother is also on the course. We run into each other in the corridor and I stop her, apologising in a very British manner for the interruption, explaining about the rucksack and asking if Jodie has indeed done the ultimate distance triathlon.

It's with an obvious mixture of pride and sadness that she says: 'Yes, Jodie did an Ironman last year and she's training for another one at the moment. But I've told her this has to be the last one. It's too much. I worry about the damage it's doing to her body.'

I nod sympathetically and ask: 'Which Ironman did she do?'

'Wales,' her mother says, her face darkening a little.

'Aha,' I say, because I've heard on the grapevine that this is one of the hardest, if not *the* hardest Ironman in the world. The events in Lanzarote and Hawaii are all about the wind and heat, but Wales is renowned for the brutality of the climbs.

'Do you think maybe Jodie might talk to me about it all?' I ask.

'Oh yes,' her mother says. 'Jodie would love to talk to you about triathlon.'

A few days later Jodie and I meet in a cafe. Although not in training gear per se, she's dressed in a sporty way, in shorts and trainers, that same Ironman rucksack on her back.

Immediately I get the impression that she is both sensitive and furiously determined, perhaps occasionally to her own detriment. She is also very direct and almost affrontingly honest. She wants to use her story to help others, she explains, as she recounts how she found triathlon the key to unlocking health after a battle with anorexia and bulimia.

'I was fifteen years old,' she says, 'when it all began to develop. I'd grown up around separation as my parents split when I was one. But when my grandparents also broke up . . . I was really close to them and now they were getting a divorce.'

One day around that time at school, somebody offered Jodie a mint, and she declined. Nobody could have predicted the result of this one simple act, nor the enormous feeling of empowerment that Jodie felt. One mint became one meal and soon Jodie was seriously undereating. Restricting food intake became a way of asserting control, she believes, and the physical manifestations of her weight loss made her smaller, more like a little girl, which she felt might bring her the protection and attention that she had found herself recently craving.

It didn't take long before Jodie, who had always been a talented sportswoman – captain of virtually every sports team in her school – developed full-blown anorexia and was unable to continue with her education. With the love and support of her family, she left school during her GCSE year and entered a rehab centre for all different types of addiction. Much like Olivia, recovery wasn't something that came to Jodie overnight. She improved, then relapsed, improved and then relapsed. But slowly she started to get well, and also to enjoy sport again. Jodie started to take an interest in nutrition and in the real purpose of food as fuel. Having been accepted back to school, where she completed her A levels, Jodie went to university to study exercise, nutrition and health, with a view to becoming better equipped to help and advise those who, like her, had suffered an eating disorder. It was in the summer of 2012, when working as an exercise specialist in a corporate environment, that she decided to give triathlon a go.

'Everybody around me seemed to be doing it so I guess I just thought, hey, why shouldn't I?'

Jodie completed a sprint-distance triathlon in Bedfordshire that September with a wetsuit she had bought a week before for £10 and a bike she had owned for just five weeks.

One year later, Jodie completed Ironman Wales. She had returned, completely unfit, from four months of travelling through China, with just four months more until the big day. There was no time to waste and, using her knowledge of nutrition to support her, Jodie immersed herself in training. Forty miles and thirty-nine hours of swimming, 1696 miles and 127 hours of cycling, and 319 miles and seventy hours of running later, Jodie ran into the sea in Tenby. Thirteen hours and eighteen minutes after the start gun went, she raced jubilantly down the final straight and crossed the finish line of what is regarded by many to be the hardest Ironman course in the world.

Perhaps this kind of fast and furious approach is what it takes to improve. I can't help but feel that, even in the rare instances where it doesn't cause long-term physical or emotional damage, it might, quite simply, be somewhat self-defeating. As always, it helps to talk my confusion through with Rob. I explain that I'm anxious I'm not doing enough, but equally anxious not to do too much and break my body, mind or both. He insists I look at the macro picture because over six months, a year or five years even, performance generally improves. That's certainly the way it goes, major injury notwithstanding, in the first few seasons of triathlon, when people tend to experience a steep improvement curve. On a smaller scale though – from week to week – progression isn't always quite so obvious. That's just life. Some weeks you feel like you're on fire, swimming well, stronger on the bike, running faster than before. But others are quite the opposite: I feel like I'm standing still or – worse – going backwards. One week in late March, for example, a horrible virus leads to a week off training and, of course, I return far quicker to my turbo sessions, using the contraption kindly lent to me by Emily, and an easy run or two before making it back to the pool. It's human nature perhaps – we do the things we like or are more naturally good at, before we do the things we need. But with triathlon this leads to a kind of exhausting frustration, which can further deplete motivation levels: *I didn't go swimming again. I should have gone swimming. Urgh. I hate swimming. I wish I didn't have to go swimming.*

(It doesn't exactly make one want to go swimming.)

As anyone who has ever trained for something knows, motivation and consistency are far harder to maintain than they are to spell. They come in waves and are particularly abundant at the beginning, when you need them the least. I might compare training for a bigger, longer event to romantic love. The first flush is gorgeous, full of energy and joy. Everything feels easy, holds great promise, and you can't imagine how it might ever not. Then, unexpectedly, things get trickier for one reason or another and there's a shift in focus or attitude. The colour drains a little from the images you conjure when you think of training/being with your lover. The opportunities seem fewer. Things that were once exciting obstacles to be overcome now look like big brick walls. You wonder if it's worth continuing at all. It all feels a little overwhelming. Maybe it's just you, but you can't help feeling it's not working. You can't remember why you began it; you start to think . . . Is it time, perhaps, just . . . to . . . stop?

The simple answer is: of course it's not. I tell myself that there are plenty of times to stop, like when you know in your soul that your body can't take any more racing, or you and your partner have arrived at the genuine end point of your relationship. But stopping mid-way? Well, that's more self-destructive than productive. The reality is that things just got a little bit tough. Isn't this what you knew would happen? Isn't this partly why you started it in the first place – to see where your mettle really lies? Whichever analogy we use, what's going on is fairly similar: you're either seeing the other person for who they really are (beyond the furies of that initial lust), or you've just jumped off your bike in a triathlon and your legs feel empty but there's a whole ten kilometres' running still to go . . .

Looking for inspiration, I start researching women I can call upon in my mind when things get tough and for reminders of the enormous benefits triathlon brings. Of course I have Jane, Ren, Paula, Suzanne and Emily, all of whom in their own way help to remind me that I can to some extent choose what is possible or not. I think often of record-breaker Diana Nyad, who in 2013 became the first swimmer to complete the 110-mile crossing from Havana, Cuba, to Key West in Florida without a shark cage. She was sixty-four at the time, it was her fifth attempt and it took about fifty-three hours, non-stop. There is also Shirin Gerami, who just a couple of weeks later, at the age of twenty-four, became the first Iranian female triathlete to take part in a World Championship, racing in the final event in the series, held in London. Gerami, who is training under Rob Popper to be a triathlon coach, knows what it is to fight for the right to participate in sport, let alone do well at it. Gerami struggled to get the go-ahead to compete from the Iranian authorities, as she told the *Guardian* a few days prior to the event: 'I wanted to share triathlon and all the empowerment it has given me, with others, and encourage others to experience and benefit from something that is dear to me.'

The message seems to be that where there's a triathlete's will, there is most definitely a way. Neither age nor cultural restraints need be a limiting factor, say the actions of both game-changers like Nyad and Gerami and women like Katharine Peters. A mother to five children who lives in south-west England and works part-time as a district nurse,

Katharine did her first super-sprint triathlon in Tockington in north Bristol. I've known her since I was very young – our brothers went to school together and our families remain close friends. It is by chance that my mother mentions Katharine's recent triathlon prowess just as I'm in need of inspiration. So I call her, a little out of the blue, and ask for the lowdown.

'It wasn't about being a triathlete for me,' she says, 'more about proving something to myself and having a focus, showing myself that I wasn't completely and utterly useless any more and could do something just for me!'

It's the quiet persistence of women like Katharine, who lost sixteen kilos in the process of training for her race, that inspires me most of all. The Whac-a-mole nature of triathlon doesn't put them off, and their commitments (five children, anyone?) are surely more demanding of their time and energy than my wife and our ginger tomcat are of mine.

10

Next comes mid April, and the Lanzarote trip, and it doesn't take long before Emily and I have a rather illuminating contretemps. It is day two and the training camp is in full swing, a group of us having just returned from a forty-kilometre ride through the island's striking volcanic land-scape. We roll our wheels through the gates of our home for the next eight days, the sport lover's paradise of Club La Santa, whose 1980s nouveau turrets loom down over an expanse of facilities: an athletics track, three Olympic pools, a lagoon and an outdoor gym.

My legs are tired but warm, my brain rested and my skin glowing from the bright overhead sun. Exercise, as reliable as ever, has left me feeling clearer and brighter. I've learned a lot during the latest session too, which almost always makes me happy. Firstly, I've been taught that leaning my weight backwards a little over the saddle on descents and continuing to pedal, albeit very gently, will help to stabilise me, and thus I'll feel a lot less terrified. Secondly, I've discovered, after a disastrous no-underwear-just-padded-shorts twenty-kilometre ride yesterday, that, contrary to popular opinion, the fully padded approach (2 × underwear, 1 × non-padded cycling shorts and 1 × padded cycling shorts on top) is far more comfortable for me on longer rides.

But I've also learned, less enjoyably, that I'm not nearly

as 'cycling fit' as I had thought. During virtually the entire ride, in fact, I lagged behind our group by about ten metres. This is, so I've been reminded on several occasions and by different people, *not* the done thing on friendly rides. In races this wind-buffering, known as drafting, is reprehensible and sometimes an offence worthy of disqualification. In the context of training rides, sticking together like little flocks of birds is regarded as a positive; the stronger ones pull along the weaker ones, shielding them from nature's force. But when the weaker ones can't quite keep up it's irritating for all concerned. Rather unkindly, it's called 'getting dropped'. And it has happened to me today, not just once but several times.

By the end, I was getting better, just about sticking with the group, albeit with a fair bit of huffing and puffing. Emily was nearer the front the whole way through and in any case I've rather given up trying to make conversation after a couple of abortive attempts when I said hello, asked a question and received a monosyllabic answer. But now, as we douse our tired legs in the club's icy leisure pool, she asks if I will be joining the group for tomorrow's ninety-kilometre ride up the island's most infamous peak: Tabayesco.

It is a relentless ten-kilometre climb, not to mention the long journey there and back, and, while I'm certainly tempted, I tell Emily no; with my first Olympic-distance triathlon in sight, not to mention lots of other training on our agenda, I'd best give tomorrow morning's cycle ride a miss in favour of something gentler, like foam rolling, a snooze and some physiotherapy exercises.

It's my first season! Give me a break! I want to yell, feeling defensive about my obvious ineptitude.

'I'm already a bit tired,' I admit.

'Well, if you stayed with the pack when you're riding, it wouldn't be so tiring,' she says.

I look twice, to check that she really meant to say this. Doesn't she realise that I was very nearly with the pack? That I didn't intend to remain ten metres behind at all times? That I haven't ridden a long way, two days in a row, like this for, well . . . ever since I can remember, actually?

'I'm doing my best,' I say.

'What are your goals for this camp?' she asks, beating the side of one hand against the palm of another.

'Goals? Like what?' I reply.

'Like,' Emily shrugs, 'swimming four hundred metres in a certain time, or knocking thirty seconds off your personal best for ten kilometres of running.'

'Oh, right.' I shake my head. My goal is to do the triathlon and survive the camp before it. 'I guess I just want to get fitter and enjoy myself.'

Silence and confusion descend in the space between us. I step out of the pool. But Emily hasn't finished: 'Those goals are vague,' she says. 'You should have smaller goals for each discipline.'

She has a point, I think, furiously, but in my hungry, tired state it's rather wasted on me.

The question is: can she tell that I'm not amused? After all, I'm really glaring at her now. But while I know that it's rare for me to look so forcefully at someone unless I'm about to kiss them (and *that* certainly isn't going to happen here), there's no reason, of course, why Emily should know that too.

I try to keep my voice quiet, my tone firm and my words concise. 'I don't need those kind of goals,' I say slowly. 'Not now. Thanks though.'

'But otherwise how will you measure improvement?' she continues, still seemingly impervious to my displeasure. 'How will you know your fitness has improved?'

I purse my lips and take a breath. We've repeatedly been told by the camp organisers that all sessions are optional, that it's supposed to be fun as well as training, and ultimately this is a 'holiday' first and foremost. The reality, however, seems somewhat different. 'Do as much or as little as you want' becomes nothing more than a mind game. The constant chatter and cajoling, the incessant talk about training translates into: do as much as it takes for you to allay your insecurities and anxieties when comparing yourself to the other obsessive-compulsive athletes.

I'm already starting to feel and resent the pressure. This isn't really Emily's fault. Nor is it caused by the intensive schedule of training that one might rightly expect from a dedicated triathlon training camp. This is about me. It's about how I react to feeling judged. It's about how I react to competition. About how I react to feeling scared.

Must think of mini goals, my brain computes. *Not trying hard enough, not pushing far enough. I should do better, seem more committed.*

Perhaps I should explain the way I feel right now – a little insecure and overtired – but in this moment I can't access humility, can't find self-confidence and have completely lost perspective. It's all I can do to stop myself from slapping the water and splashing Emily's face like a five-year-old child.

'Everyone is different,' I say, between clenched teeth.

'But you need to have –'

'No.'

There is a pause.

'I don't need your kind of goals right now,' I say, again. 'I'm here to enjoy myself, that's all.'

It is a lie, of course. Emily shrugs and dives into the pool, leaving me to head back to the sanctuary of my room to shed a furious tear or two and wonder what – just *what exactly* – I'm doing here anyway.

One week later and I'm standing on the shore at the start line of my first Olympic-distance triathlon. It is 26 April, my mother's birthday, and although she doesn't know much at all about triathlon, nor what I'm doing here, I decide to dedicate my race to her. When things get tough, I shall blow her a birthday kiss and remember home, my family; that there is a world outside all this. But there's another birthday in mind too; this is not just any old triathlon but Lanzarote's thirtieth annual Volcano Triathlon. After a humble start in 1984 with just thirty-two participants, it has grown to become a major sporting event on the island with today's start list at over three hundred.

In the seven days between my sticky conversation with Emily and the portentous calm before the race, I've come to understand why people choose to exit their regular lives and deposit themselves here for an immersive training experience. I've tried to do as much as possible in the way of training, learning and orientating, without either aggravating my injury or completely exhausting myself before the event itself, and the results, merely in distance terms, are satisfying. The last week has seen me cycle around 140 kilometres, swim at least ten and run about fifteen. It's the closest I've got to a typical triathlete's training week (albeit a little light on the running still) since I started this project.

More than that though, I've deepened my understanding of the sport as fresh challenges have inevitably arisen and unwanted mishaps have occurred. I have been moved *up* a swimming group because I was too speedy for the bottom lane; I have managed to ride with my hands down 'on the drops' (the lower part of the handlebars, deemed to be a more stable position for descending, but rather tricky for novices to get in and out of); I have done a ten-kilometre cycling 'time trial' which involved five fairly successful kilometres uphill and five painfully cautious kilometres downhill, battered by a side wind and an unexpected attack of warm rain; I have run alongside a sixty-year-old Albanian woman, Eva – a prestigious gynaecologist in her home country – who completed her first Olympic-distance triathlon here last year in just under four hours and is now back for more; I have *twice* turned up to open water practice oblivious of the fact that my wetsuit was on the wrong way round ('Um, Lucy, the zip should be at the back . . .'), and have then, once said wetsuit had been rearranged amidst my blushes, swum, shoulder to shoulder, with a wonderful Japanese man shortlisted for an adventure to the moon in 2024 – a one-way ticket, he explains, with a 0.5 per cent chance of ever returning.

I have felt elated and empowered, just as I have felt lost and longed for the security of home. I have felt both energised and exhausted, have eaten plenty of wholesome, nutrient-dense food advisable for quick recovery times, and then thrown all my knowledge aside and wolfed down chocolate as if I were in danger of wasting away. I have also missed Bella more fiercely than at almost any other time during our relationship. But we have spoken daily and both Rob and Ren have been in touch too, particularly in the lead-up to the event. Their messages have helped me more than either of them could know, and although their latest missives aren't as conflicting as they were on the eve of Tri St Lucia they are equally colourful and inspiring:

Rob:

So, three days before the race you do your last running session. Two days before the race you do your last cycling session. The day before the race, it's time for your last swimming session – make it as race specific as you can, practise putting the wetsuit on, taking it off, wear the same goggles, swim cap and tri suit as you will for the race. Then take it easy after that. You'll probably be too nervous and excited to sleep much the night before the race, don't worry about how much sleep you may or may not need, just read a book or watch a movie and rest calmly. You will be awesome, you are awesome, you have always been awesome.

Ren:

Just enjoy it, the only race you have is against yourself! You are about to embark on the next step of your adventure into the world of triathlon. Lap it up, enjoy it and go out there and fucking nail the bitch!

Perhaps the best advice I've received, however, has been from champion paratriathlete Jane Egan. I've returned to her soothing and wise words several times during the training camp, feeling protected, somehow, by her experienced and rational tone. She writes:

Don't get too carried away on the first two days and don't try to do everything – you will blow up and be unable to get the most from the camp. Pace it carefully even if you feel it seems like you should do everything. You are still in off season training so you can afford to go hard and come away tired but you don't want to miss out because you overcook it at the camp. I've watched so many age group athletes doing crazy amounts of training at camps and before a race and they too often crash and burn because it's not what they need to do at that point.

I know you have a triathlon at the end – don't get hung up on it. You are there to train and learn so you will be tired and won't be getting a proper pre-competition taper. Go into it as nothing more than an enjoyable day out with a chance to practise all the things you have been learning in a safe race situation. It's really rare to get the chance to practise and test stuff under race conditions – this is a great opportunity.

Despite her positive outlook, Jane is right that in many ways this has been the worst possible preparation for a race. Strictly speaking, one should rest or do very short, sharp sessions for the week preceding a big event, to ensure one is absolutely ready and raring to go on the start line. Instead, we've been training two or three times per day, which, as is often the case with a heavy training load where the body is placed under great stress, has made deep regenerative sleep difficult.

In another way, however, it's been the best possible introduction to the race. I've acclimatised completely to both the landscape and the heat. I've also tried swimming a few times in my wetsuit with tri suit and quick-drying sports bra underneath. I've then practised cycling in my tri suit, with and without an extra cycling top, and tested a variety of energy gels to see how they react with my fragile stomach. Perhaps most importantly of all, a friend and fellow triathlete on the camp, Leon, has helped allay my fears about the mass start by swimming over me, next to me and under me, with flailing arms and kicking legs. It wasn't nearly as bad as I had imagined; I've never felt so grateful to someone for elbowing me in the face and I have completely stopped worrying that I will drown during the swim.

I've also, rather unexpectedly, got my period. Last month it was ten days late and this month it is five days early. This early onset is quite possibly my body's reaction to the instability of being in a new place and doing a *lot* more activity than normal. For me, it isn't too serious, and I haven't skipped a period (which would be far more worrying) in years. But it remains the case that menstrual fluctuations can be a warning sign – that your complex bodily systems can't regulate the menstrual cycle because of what they perceive as a major threat, which can be anything from war to depression to endurance training or grief (arguably the endocrine system knows no difference). Our hormones have an enormous impact on how energetic or determined we feel (or not) on any given day. For professional female athletes, I suppose, this might make the crucial difference between a good performance and a winning one. For me, of course, the stakes are not so high. Nonetheless, I am thrilled; my period was due on the day of the triathlon itself, which, for obvious reasons, could have made things very difficult. Instead I've been lucky – now it has almost passed and I'm reaping the benefits: improved mood, increased energy and a higher tolerance to pain, all just in time for the big race.

But with one worry ticked off another one appears. On the eve of the race, and for the first time since we arrived over a week ago, the infamous Lanzarote wind has really picked up. There's a general 'breeze' of 24 mph forecast for race day, with gusts of 38 mph. It makes, I'm told, a kilometre feel like a mile, and it will certainly make the cycle ride in the race take longer for everyone, stripping the legs of energy and leaving them less for the run.

The goal posts have been shifted by the weather. But that's triathlon – I've learned another valuable lesson and now fully appreciate why triathletes wince a little when you ask them what their personal best time is and why Emily evaded this exact question a few months ago. Turns out her answers really weren't excuses after all – they were real and valid points, as I'm about to experience.

'Remember to enjoy it,' I whisper to myself, as if making some kind of secret deal. 'The time is irrelevant. Just empty the tank. Leave no space to wonder *what if . . .*'

I have a swim. A bike ride. And a run. Those are my three weapons. They will help me fight to the finish line and maybe today will be the day that I discover just why all the women lining up beside me are actually here. I reflect quickly on how I want this to go. It being my first Olympic distance, my main goal probably should be mere completion. But like most women drawn to triathlon, I have an ambitious side, and I've been aiming for a finish time under three hours. How this time is distributed is also important. I'm hoping, thanks to the extra buoyancy afforded by wearing a wetsuit and this week's realisation that I'm no longer a totally disastrous swimmer, that it might take just thirty minutes for the 1500-metre lagoon swim. For the forty-kilometre out-and-back bike ride, I'm thinking one hour and thirty minutes ought to do it, and I estimate a conservative fifty-five minutes for the ten-kilometre run. Then there are the two transitions, which I hope won't take more than five minutes.

Not easy, but a realistic expectation, provided nothing major goes wrong.

The gun goes – *BEAT* – and it is on. Sink? Or swim?

I wade into the lagoon, staying back and to one side, just as I'd planned.

Breathe easy, I think. *Don't panic.*

I know already that it's a dog-leg-shaped course, marked by huge yellow buoys, but still I have to look up every few strokes to see where I am. Limbs splash about every which way, pink swim caps bobbing around like mini-buoys as I try to power forward, not allowing myself to be disturbed or slowed down by the occasional stroke, slap or nudge from another swimmer.

It's hard to get into a rhythm. About a quarter of the way through I look up and notice, with disappointment, how many swim caps are ahead. A little further on I feel myself being continuously nudged by another swimmer so decide to roll onto my back, move out of their way and take a deep, calming breath. It is now that I realise, incredulously, how many swimmers are also behind me. I had imagined myself bringing up the rear like I had in Tri St Lucia, but in fact I'm somewhere in the middle of the pack. Enlivened by this knowledge I roll back onto my front and start front crawl with noticeably more purpose. Very soon I have arrived at the first buoy. Turn right, swim for around two hundred metres and then I'm at the second. Minutes pass and at last I can see the flags waving that mark the end of the swim. I emerge onto the shore and wander haphazardly up one hundred metres of temporary red carpet and into the transition area. When I arrive I see that the bicycles that were racked next to mine are gone. They belong to the various female members of our training camp taking part in the race, including Emily, who has worked very hard on her swimming, doing around eight kilometres per week over the past few months. She has risen in the dark before dawn many times this winter and cycled to Hyde Park to swim in the freezing water of the Serpentine. She has swum endless laps in the pool during evening sessions. And now all those hours have paid off; I suspect she is already on her bike before I've even removed my goggles.

Standing beside my bike, I try, in vain, to take my wet-suit off. The last and only time I seriously practised this was more than four weeks ago during a monthly training session with Rob. After a panicked text from me telling him that my wetsuit simply didn't fit, he generously found a gap in his diary in which to painstakingly go through the motions, showing me that there are ways to put wetsuits on and Ways to Put Wetsuits On. You don't just yank it on and hope for the best, as I had originally done. Rather, you should gently pull at your legs, just like you would when putting tights on. Then you pull the material up and up, over the torso, then grab the shoulder and tug it on, and over, and on and over . . . This will give you much more space to breathe. Then you need to bend over and take hold of the stomach area of the suit and pull it up. Taking it off, Rob had explained patiently, can also be done in various ways. You can try the *just get the thing off any which way*, as I've done each time I've worn it out here in Lanzarote, or you can do it the meas-ured, tactical way that he showed me, which I now cannot for the life of me remember.

Today I've got the first bit right – pop one hand behind one's back and grab the tag and pull until the zip comes undone – and then pulled the arms off by grabbing a hand-ful of each shoulder with the opposite hand and pulling out the offending arm in a kind of 'ta-DA!' motion before doing the same on the other side. But now, instead of doing what I was taught – i.e. *not* bending over and thus shunting the blood around the body and inducing yet more dizzi-ness, but instead standing on the material discarded from your torso and 'stepping' it off – I'm lying on the ground, pulling at the legs and muttering expletives to myself.

It takes four minutes and thirty-three seconds after exiting the water before I leave transition on my bike. Once the wetsuit was finally removed, there were feet to be dried off and popped into cycling shoes, a helmet to put on, some water to be drunk and . . .

It is possibly the most exhausting and humiliating part of the whole race. I'll discover later that the top woman whizzed through T1 in just over two minutes and that the average time in this first transition was just under three. Now, and only now, do I understand why Rob kept telling me to be that athlete who actually *cares* about transitions.

What seems like hours later, and already sweating from the wetsuit ordeal, I start my cycle ride. It begins with a significant climb out of Club La Santa and up into the nearby village of Sóo. It's about ten kilometres in total before I cycle through the village of Famara. As I ride away from it, the ocean appears on my left. The wind is really noticeable now. It blows pieces of the beach – sand and debris – across the road so that it gathers dangerously in little clumps, hazardous for fast, unwary tyres.

The sand slips beneath my sunglasses and prickles at my eyes. Having been flanked by one cyclist or another for most of the ride thus far, I suddenly find myself alone. No longer am I able to play my favourite game of waiting for the person behind to overtake and then, when they are right alongside me, putting on a spurt of speed, forcing them to either go really hard to pass me or drop back completely (such is the strict 'no drafting' rule in this race that they can't tuck in just behind). I ride, lonely, around the corner and begin what I know will be a long, steady climb up to the turn point – a roundabout – some nine or ten kilometres away. As I ascend, the man in first place – the leader of the entire race, in fact – passes on the other side of the road.

But he's not moving nearly as fast as I would expect, obviously cycling straight into the wind. I, on the other hand, have it directly behind me, a huge relief from the side wind I've tackled on and off until this point.

The mid-morning sun beats down on my skin. In a moment of vanity, I pull my sleeves up a little, hoping to get the smoothest tan possible. It is the closest I come in the entire race – the entire week, in fact – to falling off my bike. I don't think anybody sees, though on the other side of the road the more serious triathletes are passing in droves. I'm cheered, for a moment, by the sight of a face I know from our training camp. It's Siv, a female member of the Norwegian army who has booked this camp in a determined attempt to yank her fitness up in readiness for the Norseman Ironman (Ren's 'bucket list' race) in August. She is a very strong cyclist, has done every single training session and looks as if she could crush my arm with one hand. Yet even Siv is struggling.

'My God! This wind, argh!' she screams to a fellow cyclist as she overtakes.

It doesn't look pretty. Each and every one passes with elbows bent and back curved to ensure the minimum resistance. Their faces growl with pain.

'Where is Emily?' I think, remembering Ren's implicit challenge that I beat her or die trying.

No sign. Kilometres pass. Ren will be disappointed but I don't care. I'm going as hard as I can, as hard as my physical and mental training thus far will allow. I call to mind Jane's advice to enjoy it. That's how I want today to go. The gradient flattens out and for a few hundred metres I cruise along a fast, flat stretch. Soon I see the race marshals smiling and waving flags, controlling the traffic, as I approach the roundabout that marks the mid point of the ride. It's down-hill now. Halfway through the ride means halfway through the three portions of the race. But just as I turn, I hear a rush of sound – like an angry snarl – which is quickly suc-ceeded by the sense that something, or someone, is pushing me backwards.

The headwind. I reach into my back pocket and rip an energy gel open with my teeth, smiling as I suck down every last saccharine, synthetic drop. The game is on. Rather un-expectedly, I feel a surge of wonderful, unadulterated power and happiness: I am here. I'm doing a triathlon. My first Olympic-distance triathlon. And I'm appreciating it, sa-vouring the privilege of being able to push my head, heart and muscles. There's a kind of super-reality to it, as if I'm watching myself from a pocket of swift-moving Canary Is-land cloud. My thoughts can now commandeer my experi-ence of each single precious moment. Sure, there's negativ-ity, which hammers at my head and tells me I'm slow, or weak, or tired. Yet I don't welcome it, trying instead to focus on what's actually going on inside me, on the beautiful, al-most Neanderthal simplicity of competition, ambition and might. It's an enviable place to be, though the pain of get-ting there is not.

The wind having robbed me of some speed, it is one hour and thirty-seven minutes since sitting on its saddle that I am rolling the wheels of my bike back over the line into transition. In an attempt to make up for my uselessness in the previous transition, I've already taken my helmet off and am running towards a woman wearing a bib and holding a clipboard.

'Putyourhelmeton!' She fires words at me in a Spanish accent.

'What? Why?' I'm bemused.

'The rules.'

A vague memory returns to me. Something about how you have to keep your helmet on until after you've racked your bike.

Shit.

I pop it back on my head, crossly.

'Do it up,' she barks.

It's clear that I have to actually do up the clasp under my chin. It doesn't matter that I am off my bike and won't be getting back on it today. Her face says it all: rules are rules; we can stand here all day if you like, Englishwoman.

I do what I'm told and get on with it. Yet again, I'm faced with the disheartening reality that my compadres are ahead, their bikes already in a neat row next to mine, including – I take a moment to check – yes, Emily's too. She is, literally, on the run, and I haven't a second more to lose.

Another energy gel, a sip of water, cycling shoes off, running shoes on, and I begin the third and final leg of this race. The first couple of hundred metres are fairly torturous; my feet feel as if they've never before trodden on ground. But quickly something shifts and I'm pleasantly surprised by how sprightly I feel. This is nothing like Tri St Lucia and the dead legs I ran with there, maybe because it's significantly cooler and I haven't been ill the night before. Or maybe, just maybe, I'm actually fitter. Whatever the cause, I'm happy with the effect, and seem to be overtaking people as I make progress on the two-lap out-and-back run course down to La Santa village. At one point I actively slow myself down a little, keen to hold something back and not risk hitting a wall too early. It's not that I'm *not* hurting (of course I am, I've just swum fifteen hundred metres and ridden forty kilometres, and now I'm running, for goodness' sakes), it's just that I know this hurt, it's a bearable, almost pleasurable hurt, rather than anything threatening or more sinister.

There she is, coming towards me in a bright red Hong Kong tri suit, on the return journey of her first lap as I'm on the outward journey of mine.

'Go, Emily!' I yell. 'Bravo!'

She looks up and our eyes meet. I'm sure she's seen me.

She looks down again. Runs on, without a word.

And then there's no more hanging back. I know I've little chance of catching her (she must be two kilometres ahead) but I can at least narrow the space between us. I return to Club La Santa, run once around the track and then exit it for my second lap. Five kilometres to go and from that moment on it's pure survival. Counting down tiny landmarks. This leaning tree, that wonky piece of pavement . . . It's all one landmark closer to the finish. I think of Ren now, and her Ironman. How she ran four times this distance, after a much longer swim and an endless, brutal ride. I think too of Jane Egan, and the unimaginable challenge of swimming, cycling and running through near-constant and agonising neural pain.

Just don't stop, Fry, I tell myself, using my surname, as Ren would, for emphasis. *Don't stop your legs. One foot. In front. Of another. When you think you can't run faster, just try. And try and try and try.*

I hear myself wheezing; I hear myself swear. Along the way, I holler encouraging words at those I know, like my new friend Sarah, who goes on to win her age group. I give the thumbs up to those I don't know, and I pass people I vaguely recognise because they passed me on the bike. Up one last hill and, nearly there, I put on one final spurt of speed before re-entering the club's four-hundred-metre track, driving my arms forward and back in a sprinting motion before crossing the finish line.

11

Lanzarote training camp: done. Olympic distance: done. I feel invincible for days afterwards, as if all the new experiences and achievements are coins thrown into a piggy bank of confidence. Swim 1500 metres in race conditions? Tick! Ride against the wind and still feel strong? Tick! Run ten kilometres with legs beaten by a forty-kilometre ride in tough conditions? Tick! During the week immediately after, I wander around south London with a mind hijacked by memories. Sipping coffee at my favourite cafe, mid-way through typing an email, I find myself back in Lanzarote, riding into that headwind or gasping for breath in the lagoon. In hindsight, it looks even better than it felt at the time. My heart bursts with pride. I have surprised myself with what is possible. Negativity has a little bit less power. Nobody – especially not me – can tell me with ease that there is something I just can't do.

But there is, of course, a physical pay-off. Despite my increased motivation, I also come home exhausted. I know that only rest, a little yoga and the right kind of food will help me recover after such an intense ten days' activity. My brain wants to train but my body does not. During my downtime I consider my performance, recalling the clock above my head as I crossed the finish line in three hours, three minutes and two seconds. I've accepted the three minutes over three hours now, my disappointment tempered by the fact that everybody agreed the cycle ride was approximately fifteen minutes longer than it might have been on a more forgiving course. I am also, I'll admit, relieved that Emily only managed a finishing time of two hours, fifty-six minutes and three seconds: a mere six minutes and fifty-nine seconds (no, that's not the same as seven minutes) less than me. There is nothing like a friendly rival to focus the mind on one's performance. I jot down the differences in our respective results and question myself as to where and how I can improve. Emily's swim was almost four minutes faster than mine and her first transition a minute and a half less than my galumphing effort. Her bike ride wasn't even two minutes quicker than mine, my second transition was twenty seconds longer than hers and my run over half a minute faster, though both of us managed under fifty minutes for ten kilometres.

Out of a field of seventy-four women, including professionals, Emily and I managed a fairly respectable twenty-fourth and thirty-third place respectively. Well done us, I think, but there is another statistic, less easy on the eye, that's of interest: out of the 308 entrants in Volcano Tri, only those seventy-four were female, as opposed to 234 men. Female participation in this event has risen over the last decade at least; where women made up approximately one sixth of the field in 2004 they now account for around a quarter. But still . . . Am I the only one who wants to see equal numbers in triathlon? What is it in particular about this sport that causes such a marked disparity? It isn't this way with all mass participation events: more than fifty per cent of those who ran that half marathon with me last September were

female. In the five-kilometre, untimed Color Run race series, an American import that's popping up all around the
UK, about eighty per cent are female. In general, the events
where women dominate are those, like Mud Runs and as-
sault courses, where finishing times are less important than
having fun. Is it the uncompetitive nature of the event that
draws them in droves? The run portion of a sprint distance is
no longer than five kilometres, and women are generally on
a level with men when it comes to swimming. So perhaps it
is the cycling in triathlon that puts off so many women. Or,
rather, the cycling only appeals to the particularly physically
tough women who aren't easily intimidated.

Looking at the winners of the 2014 Lanzarote Volcano
Triathlon, there is a marked disparity in female and male cycling times in particular. Spaniard Saleta Castro (age group
25–29) won overall in the female race in two hours, twenty
minutes and nineteen seconds. This comprised a swim of
twenty-two minutes and sixteen seconds, a first transition
of two minutes and nine seconds, a cycle of one hour, fifteen minutes and thirty-three seconds, a fifty-two-second
transition from bike to run, and a run of thirty-nine minutes and thirty-one seconds. The male winner, Frenchman
Romain Guillaume (also in the 25–29 age bracket), won
in a super-speedy one hour, fifty-eight minutes and fifteen
seconds, 114 seconds faster than the Belgian man who came
in at number two. Guillaume's swim time was eighteen minutes and fifty-four seconds (a *very* impressive 1500-metre
swim time), his first transition was one minute and fifty-one
seconds, his cycle time one hour, two minutes and eleven
seconds, his second transition just forty-seven seconds, and

his run time thirty-four minutes and thirty-four seconds. So yes, he was faster over all parts of the race than the female winner, Castro. But it was his cycling that really set them apart from one another.

Is there any kind of logic to all of this? It is part physiology, so coaches have told me during the training camp in Lanzarote. A solid power-to-weight ratio is very important on the bike and far less so on the swim. Is this why, according to Rob, there are far more male cyclists than female cyclists at club level? The numbers for men and women in running and swimming clubs are far more equal, he says, adding that there's also the psychology of training – there are more aggressive, competitive 'A-type' men who enter triathlons to 'prove a point, or smash the opposition', whereas women tend to get involved for health, fitness and enjoyment. Interestingly, Rob also suggests that the preconceptions surrounding triathlon – that one needs to be lean, hardcore, a sports fanatic to become involved – put off women more than they put off men. As to why *that* is? It is a whole other set of suppositions, a whole other story, perhaps, but there are semantics for a start: Ironman races, although a nod to the generic term for mankind (which also pertains to a certain patriarchal linguistic structure, of course), are named in a way that certainly suggests one must be not boy, not girl, not woman, but man to try it out. But there is something else here – we women are far more complicit in our own denigration than we often realise or like to admit. Standing on the start line of various sporting events I have learned one thing: the majority of non-elite sportswomen feel the need to play down their sporting ambitions and achievement and feel easily intimidated by high expectations. It is as if they feel their very womanhood is threatened if they display the kind of alpha, competitive 'I'm going to do my best, be pugnacious and compete' attitude that we have come to associate with men, masculinity or manhood.

It makes me sad, frustrated and a little bit ashamed. If you don't want to compete, at whatever level, then don't. If you do, then do. But for God's sake don't make the mistake of thinking it has anything whatsoever to do with your gender, or that anybody important will consider how high you set your sights, or how hard you push, the mark of femininity, masculinity, or both.

Of course there are many women who defy these generalisations. Women who train with and compete against men, pro triathlete women such as Chrissie Wellington who, although not particularly tall or big, routinely finished in the top ten overall in her races. I think also of Jodie, whose struggles with food were helped by triathlon and who prefers to train with men because she finds the typical female attitude to enduring pain a bit too wimpy. Suzanne, too, has beaten many men in Ironman races, and started out, just as Jodie has, in a field of swimmers made up predominantly of more powerful, heavier men.

Beyond the clear gulf between elite and non-elite, and beneath any obvious gender differences, I wonder what typical characteristics might remain. Limitless dedication seems to be fairly prevalent across the board and is in keeping with the frustrations that Rob has spoken to me about; that getting triathletes to rest, recover and repair is far harder than getting them to train. As he tells me in an email:

The negative side of this can be a certain obsessiveness: a fascination with mileage and over-attention to quantitative training, thinking that it is de facto better to swim 10K, cycle 200K or run 50K in a week, regardless of the quality of the training. Once upon a time, I would have said this was much more of a male trait, with women more focused on quality versus quantity, but that is not so clearly the case any more.

But there are other, quirkier, elements more specific to triathlon, Rob writes, many of which I recognise already, even after such a small amount of time invested in the sport:

Triathletes can be gadget-obsessed and metric-obsessed. They measure everything, record everything, compare everything, tweet everything. On the positive side, this can help people focus on their own personal gains and stay motivated for years and years. On the negative side, this can make us triathletes very dull at parties and family occasions, never shutting up about all the different things we have measured this week. Again, this used to be much more of a male thing, but I now see almost as many women fascinated with their gadgets as men.

'Yes!' I think, remembering the wattage meter Ren had on her bike when I did my turbo session and the mileage counter she had when we went riding together in the Surrey hills.

Triathletes also tend to be very well-rounded people. Again, you kind of have to be if you are going to tackle a multi-sport like this. This usually means that your average triathlete is a well-educated, open-minded person with a wide range of interests and probably has some interesting stories to tell. It also means we tend to have a jack-of-all-trades approach to things, not mastering any one discipline.

'Maybe . . .' I reflect. But I'm not convinced. So far I think I've seen more obsessive than well rounded.

Triathletes can be quite tough, in a mental-toughness kind of way. ['No doubt about that,' I think.] We seem to take a great deal of pride in doing things other 'ordinary' people don't, won't or can't do. For example, open water swimming requires a certain kind of mental toughness, especially if you are swimming in a 13-degree-cold lake in Essex at 7 a.m. on a Saturday (which might mean getting up at 5.30 a.m. so you can meet up with some friends and cycle out to said lake, and then cycle back when you are done). This can lead to a certain kind of quiet machismo, which is not always a bad thing, not always a good thing, just depends on which way you want to go with it and how much you crow about it to other people.

Machismo, yes. Quiet, no. The crowing is everywhere.

Triathletes can also be very kind, helpful, friendly, altruistic people. I've seen and heard more examples of triathletes helping each other out than I have of triathletes being mean or nasty with each other. Lots of free advice, plenty of people willing to lend their equipment for free.

'Absolutely my experience,' I think. 'Emily lent me her turbo, Ren has given her time and energy and Rob his expertise. This community expands to fill the space it's given.'

Which of those characteristics have I developed during the past six months, I wonder? I am not yet obsessed by gadgets, nor mileage, probably because I don't need to see on screen that I haven't done enough. I would say I was well rounded in that I have a mixture of training, work and love in my life, but that balance has previously been something I've swung past on my way from one extreme to another, whereas this year I'm increasingly keen to master it. Yes, I think I can be tough mentally, but if I were to compare myself to Ironwomen – Jodie, Ren or Suzanne perhaps – I have no doubt that I would fall short. But again, that's a matter of degree, and opinion. One person's obsession is another person's inspiration; one woman's crazy is another woman's average Sunday morning.

No – the least subjective common denominator I have found amongst triathletes is that we are all striving, active and conscious participants in the journey of bettering ourselves and discovering what lies across the threshold of muscular pain and mental endurance. How such betterment actually arrives – for some it is via freezing early-morning swims, for others via mastering their fear on a bicycle going downhill – doesn't even matter. Triathlon is triumph over fear, and triathletes concern themselves with the business of conquering fear. It isn't so much about speed as ignoring the natural desire to take it easy and slow down. In this way the sport is an insurance policy against an uninvigorating, unchallenging life. It is about choosing to swim instead of sink. About fumigating your body and brain of the stench of apathy.

It's also about just getting the hell on with things. There's no way that all the necessary swim, bike and run training sessions, not to mention strength training, yoga or the various other things plenty of triathletes squeeze into their weeks and months, can get done off the back of pure desire all the time. Motivation is hard to keep alive; even Ren admitted to me once that it is something she struggles with, and that training with a triathlon club is really her only way of holding herself consistently accountable to her own goals. Don't imagine for one second that all those committed to, and inspired by, triathlon always find it easy to stay on track. There must be a superior incentive that keeps them focused. This is usually something they have visualised over and over and which they want more than a lie-in, an extra beer or that city break in New York. For Ren I think it's that desire to separate herself from the ordinary, something Rob has now mentioned too. For Suzanne and Emily I think it's about sharing a certain outdoorsy lifestyle and keeping their bodies fit enough that they can see the world in the loudest, proudest way. For Jodie this macro-motivation is as specific as one significant race. Everything she's doing this year, the extra hours spent training, isn't just to conquer Ironman Wales. She did that last year. No, it's to beat other female competitors in her age group (18–24) and thus be automatically awarded the chance to race at one of the most coveted events in the entire triathlon world: Ironman Kona Hawaii. Jodie knows as well as any professional athlete that big dreams are made of small pieces, laid upon one another bit by bit, and this summer every session counts.

Jodie has an overwhelming need to prove something to

the world and to herself. And though she is far more independent, there's much about Jodie's driving insecurity that reminds me of my younger self – the youthful warrior, full of hubris and enthusiasm. I really believe that she can win her age-group category in this race. There is one competitor, however, who might stand in Jodie's way and that is twenty-three-year-old Hollie Cradduck, who last year finished next after Jodie in the 18–24 age group. As Hollie crossed the finish line of her first ever Ironman, Wales, she received the news that her nineteen-year-old niece Rosie was dead. Rosie had suffered an epileptic fit during the night and by the time family members found her, Hollie was already racing. They decided nothing would be gained from pulling Hollie out halfway through, but, her suspicion already aroused by the stony faces of her supporters, she knew as soon as she crossed the line: something serious was wrong. Overwhelmed by shock and grief, Hollie soon decided: next year she would win her age group and get the coveted place at Kona, raising money along the way for a charity (SUDEP) researching ways of preventing Sudden Unexpected Death in Epilepsy. Since then she has been training furiously hard.

'I feel a bit guilty about wanting to beat her,' Jodie admits, as we sit talking in a central London cafe. After everything Hollie has suffered it's an understandable reaction. Chasing dreams involves sacrifices of all kinds, I reflect, including going against one's better nature. So what are mine? I want, more than anything, to come away from this year in triathlon with a set of experiences I won't forget and a fresh understanding of the hypnotic elements of the sport. But I also want to stay intact, emotionally and mentally. I want to grow rather than diminish that sense of self-acceptance that has begun to develop since I slipped over from my twenties into my thirties. Already I stand just a little taller in the pub, because I know that maintaining good posture is the best counterbalance to the damage done through hours of cycling. I buy fewer drinks, partly because I consume mostly water now, as I'm forever in between training sessions, and partly because I've tightened the purse strings in the knowledge that I'll need more money to fund my newfound, albeit slightly healthier, habit. In some circles they call this 'cross-addiction'. In triathlon it is just normal. So, sure, I'm a triathlete now, but it isn't exactly the fully soulful, life-altering, immersive experience that I had anticipated. Nor has it left me, as it has many of my friends, completely obsessive about triathlon. Yes, my confidence in my body and its resilience and abilities has increased. Yes, I have learned that it is just as difficult and gruelling as it sounds, putting three sports one after the other and calling it a race. And yes, I'm well aware now that energy gels make the difference between a horrific long slog and a rewarding, teeth-gnashing effort.

But really, is that what I started this for? And if I don't feel different now, when will I? Perhaps after the three next triathlons, I will have caught the bug and not look back. Or maybe it really changes in one's second season, but will I finish the first with any intention to continue? I'll have to wait and see. There is one thing, though, that has taken me by surprise: I am both aghast and thrilled at how much I have begun to get out of swimming, and that in turn has taught me one vital lesson: you think you know yourself, but you don't. Give everything a decent shot; take lessons before you give up; only losers pigeonhole themselves.

~~●~~

It is in exactly this spirit that I decide to stop questioning and act. There is much to be done. I have just over four weeks until the next triathlon, in Hyde Park, and not more than five until the following one at Blenheim.

During the month of May, I find a groove with my training, consistently managing five or six sessions a week and ensuring that each is purposeful, geared specifically towards the sprint triathlons coming up. I head to Shepperton Lake outside London with swim coach friend Salim to work through sighting drills – lifting one's head or eyes to orientate oneself without stopping. I start running regularly again, a little hill training on Streatham Common, just once a week to stave off further injury. I manage two one hundred-kilometre rides on consecutive weekends. One is with Ren, a flat ride from home to Windsor and back, and one an organised mass participation event. The former is tiring but fun and we are back by lunchtime. The latter takes longer and also more out of my body. It is perhaps more useful, however, in that I experience for the first time what it is like to properly run out of steam on a bicycle. After not eating or drinking much for the first three hours, I begin to feel weak and decrepit, as if an all-pervasive melancholy had overtaken both my thighs and my thoughts. At the second fuel station (I stupidly rode on past the first, deeming it unnecessary after just ninety minutes), I drain a gallon of water and munch two flap-jacks. Within two minutes I feel so sure I have sprouted wings that I almost turn to a fellow cyclist and ask him if he could take a picture of them for me to add to Facebook when I get home.

I also meet Rob in Regent's Park one hot and sticky Thursday lunchtime for a brick session.

'Sorry, I've had a horrible ride through nasty traffic to get here,' I say, explaining my lateness and discernible stress.

One look at Rob's kind smile and I feel calmed. I'm sure that like all of us Rob has his fair share of anxiety, trauma and self-doubt going on, but when I'm around him I feel an overwhelming sense of safety. Like everything, everywhere, is going to be all right so long as we all keep meeting up for cycle rides and drinking high-quality coffee.

We cycle into the middle of the park's Inner Circle and stop to rest our bikes against a hedge.

'Right,' says Rob. 'It's exactly one kilometre around this circular road. So you're going to cycle a lap. Then come and put your bike against the wall, *then and only then* take your helmet off, change out of your cycling shoes into your run-ning shoes and off you go. Running around for a lap. Then bike. Then run. Two or three times, we'll see how you are feeling. I'll stay here and time you.'

He holds up his hand to reveal a stopwatch. It's black and fits inside his palm, with a button on the top that his fore-finger hovers over.

'Old skool,' I laugh.

He smiles. 'I'm going to time each lap and your transi-tions. We're not aiming for crazy speed here but consistency.'

Ah. Consistency. Rob has located my Achilles heel and named it already.

The first lap flies by, as it should really, given that it's only a kilometre and I have two wheels to help me transport my body across the distance. Before I know it I'm approaching a slim figure, dressed in casual sports gear and a trendy cycling cap, formerly known as Rob but now just appearing to me as the Timer. It's like being a real athlete with a real chance of qualifying for something! I say little as I bring the bike in ('Doing great,' says Rob, pressing a button on the stopwatch). Next I descend, remove helmet, swap shoes and ('Not bad,' he says: 'fourteen seconds for transition . . .') head off on the run.

After three trips each on both bike and feet with, according to Rob, some 'decent pacing', we decide to get some lunch, cruising north on our bicycles over Primrose Hill and into a nearby cafe. We order eggs and coffee and I learn that Rob has two children, a twenty-two-year-old son and sixteen-year-old daughter who were only nine and three when he started triathlon.

'It was a source of joking around,' he says. 'You know: what does Dad want for Christmas? Easy! Anything to do with swimming, cycling and running. Or, rolling eyes: Dad, it's 5.30 a.m., are you seriously going for a swim now?'

'So you were obsessed?'

'Yeah, kinda,' he says. 'I mean, it was a total transformation, but one which happened quite gradually. From 2001, when I started training, to 2010, when I became a full-time coach, the physical and social changes were quite profound. On several levels, I saw triathlon as the answer to all of life's problems and put myself in a very different space than I had been in before starting down that road. Getting old and tired? Take up triathlon! Feeling unfit and flabby? Take up triathlon! Not earning enough money? Do some triathlon coaching on the weekends.'

But it wasn't just weekends. Eventually Rob's tri coaching took over and, although he still runs the small non-profit website consultancy and training company that he set up long ago, it became a full-time job.

'It's very tough,' he says. 'Bottom line: work in the sports industry and it'll generally pay terribly. Even when you pay some top trainer £100 or more, you have to understand the time and expense behind that one hour they are giving you and the maximum any individual can deliver in one week.'

During the time we've known each other I've never really asked Rob how he feels about his job. I've merely assumed that because he clearly loves triathlon, he is fulfilled as a coach.

'It is emotionally rewarding,' he goes on, 'but very draining work too. Not just the early mornings and evening sessions but also, the better your trainer or coach is, the more they are going to put of themselves into each session and the harder that is to repeat and sustain. Well, it is for me anyway.'

I wait.

'In my effort to achieve balance in my life and build something more substantial than an hour-by-hour, week-by-week pattern, I need to find some other kind of work to balance out the tri coaching. It's my joy, my passion, my pride . . . but it would kill me and bankrupt me if I let it.'

'Wait,' I say, just to be clear: 'So you're not going to carry on doing what you're doing? With triathlon coaching I mean?'

He holds his cup in his hands and shrugs. 'I mean . . . I'll always do it, even if it's just part-time. But this lifestyle, and this money? It's simply not sustainable.'

By mid May the dividends of the training I did in Lanzarote are really beginning to pay off. I've been waiting for this! I remember our head coach on the camp, ex-professional triathlete Richard Hobson, saying I should feel the camp's full effects around three weeks after. We were cycling next to one another at the time, just before he shot off ahead to join a faster group. I decide to email him now for a little clarification. Just why am I suddenly feeling a surge in fitness *now*, so long after I've returned to the UK?

He replies:

That whole thing about taking three weeks to feel the full effect of training in Lanzarote isn't really an exact science. It totally comes down to how hard you have trained and run yourself down, for how long you have done so (1 week/2 weeks etc), how old you are, how quickly you recover generally along with a few other factors. But it is normally about the time that it takes me to recover. It relates to the basic principle of training which is that the body supercompensates after a period of training – so actually we do not get fitter when we train; we get fitter when we recover from the training. But supercompensation really is

an individual thing and does depend on the factors mentioned
above.

Aha! All is revealed. Without knowing it I have timed
things impeccably. Thanks to ten days' training far tougher
than my usual regime and the resulting supercompensation
I am feeling primed and ready, my third triathlon on the
horizon, just under a week away.

12

But what goes up must come down, goes the old adage, and in the days preceding the Hyde Park Triathlon I am feeling strangely fatigued and low. Rob recommends I give Sunday's race a miss and focus my efforts on the one I've planned for next Saturday instead.

'Two races within six days is pushing it,' he advises gently.

I politely ignore him. Not because I think he's wrong (quite the opposite, in fact), but because, while it's far from ideal that they are less than one week apart, I really don't want to miss out on either race. The first I'm excited about because it's in my home town of London and is part of the World Series. This means I'll be swimming, cycling and running in the same water and on the same roads as the professionals will have done the day before and which Ren and Emily trod in last year's event.

This year, however, Ren will be on the other side of the lines to shout at various friends taking part, including me. Over coffee a couple of days before, she's given me very direct instructions as to how I should *attack* the race.

'Apparently, when you get in the water, there are some secret steps somewhere. If you can line up near those, then you can push yourself off and get a big head start.'

I nod sagely, though I'm under no illusions a) that I'll remember or be able to find the secret steps, or b) that it would make more than half a second's difference to my swim time. It'll be my first time starting a triathlon actually *in* the water, and doing so in water – the Serpentine – that I've never swum in before.

'Don't worry if there's a bit of jostling at the start,' she continues. 'You'll be taller and stronger than most of the girls there, so if someone hits you, just hit them back. That's why triathletes swim like this . . .' She makes a flailing motion with one arm, bringing it out to one side and then moving it, fast, back towards the centre. No doubt about it: it might look nothing like good freestyle swim technique, but if that arm slapped against someone, it would hurt.

'Taller and *stronger*?' I say.

Has Ren just given me a compliment?

I almost fall off my chair in the overpriced central London juice bar we're sitting in.

'Just fight back, Fry,' she says.

'Yeah, I might just do that.'

'Then don't fuck up your transition,' Ren tells me. 'Ride hard, and really run. It's a sprint, Fry, remember that.'

Again I nod. Of course, we both know it's not a real sprint – that's something one can't actually maintain for more than about twenty seconds – but I know what she's getting at. She means no holding back, no saving energy *just in case.*

And that preys on my mind, a lot, as time ticks away until the race.

No holding back.

Attack.

Just go as hard and fast as you can, for around one and a half hours of your life.

I can anticipate – almost taste – the way that hurts. Will I be able to dig deep this time, the way I didn't really bother to in St Lucia, and push through physical pain to knock my sprint distance performance, perhaps quite literally, out of the water?

In the hours directly before the race I'm inspired by news from Jane. Not only has she won yesterday's Hyde Park Paratriathlon but she did so by a huge seven-minute margin.

The water was cold, between 15 and 16 degrees, so be ready for that, she says in a message. *Once you are going it's no problem, just the initial shock!*

It's with Jane's fabulous victory in mind that I pack my things up – *wetsuit, swimcap, goggles, spare goggles, brightly coloured towel (to help me identify my bike), race belt (with main race number attached), timing chip* – and give them to Bella to take to Hyde Park. Next I eat a large plate of eggs on toast washed down with strong coffee and water. I spend a little time looking over the course map in the competitors' information guide, in an attempt to familiarise myself with the twists and turns of the cycle course, and put my race number stickers on my helmet and bike.

Have I got everything?

I check several times. Then check one more time, just to be sure, before finally getting dressed in my quick-drying sports bra, tri suit and cycling top. Helmet and sunglasses safely on, I set off on my bike into central London.

Bella and I meet in the park forty-five minutes later and stroll over to a quiet spot so I can put my waterproof timing chip around my ankle and have a drink. It's a beautiful summer's day, warm and dry, after a week of almost solid rain. My start time – 14.40 – is imprinted on my mind. But first I must head over to the transition area to rack my bike. One by one, I tick things off, checking and double-checking that everything is prepared:

Cycling shoes out. With velcro straps open so I can slip my wet feet easily into them.

Running shoes out. With socks all ready and special laces that don't need to be tied, so I can get them on quicker, and without shaking-hand time-heavy lace-tying disasters.

Cycling top out. My choice; you can ride and run in just a tri suit on warm days like this but I feel more comfortable this way.

Helmet and sunglasses out.

Water bottles full, and in their holsters on my bike.

Check, check, check.

Yes, it's all here. Thirty minutes to go. The only thing that's left is to find and greet my father, who has come along to lend a photographic hand and give support. Once I've done that I'll simply need to put on my wetsuit and swim cap and plonk some goggles on my head.

'Hey!' yells Bella, through the mesh fence that separates competitors from spectators. 'Don't you need that band thingy around your wrist?'

I look down.

Panic: the band that lets me in and out of transition. It isn't on my wrist. I know, immediately, that it's at home on the kitchen table. Somehow I've slipped through into the transition area unnoticed, but when it comes to the race I'll be blocked if I don't have this plastic bracelet on.

Sheepishly, I head over to a friendly marshal and explain. Thankfully it's no big deal: I manage to get a replacement and all's well again. But it's not been a helpful interlude; I can feel my heart beat harder and faster under my skin.

Twenty minutes later and I'm lining up with the other orange swim caps, ready to start. Competitors are going off every ten minutes in waves of fifty. We huddle together and try to listen to the pre-race briefing. It's useless – the sound of a man talking into a microphone as other competitors cross the nearby finish line deafens me and I hear virtually nothing of the instructions that, I gather, are about various bits of the course.

'It'll be all right,' says a woman lining up alongside me, when I say that I haven't the faintest clue if what that man just said was important. 'You just follow the person in front.'

I am neither hurt nor flabbergasted that she has assumed I won't be leading the pack. I am, however, slightly irritated. What does she know? I could be an ex-county swimmer, a freestyle master hidden in a very thick middle-of-the-range wetsuit.

We walk up the pier – though right now it feels more like a gangplank – and, upon instruction, drop down into the water.

The nerves gather around me like bubbles.

'One hand on the side please,' says the steward.

We can't let go until the horn goes: *PRRRRRRRRRRNNN-NNNNNNN.*

It sounds like a boat, warning of its impending arrival. Everybody releases the side and starts swimming. I decide to try to swim hard from the off, breathing every two strokes instead of every three. Because I've nabbed the starting spot right at the end of the row, there are no issues whatsoever with other people, no need to *hit back* as Ren insisted I must. What is problematic, however, is the small explosion that's taking place inside my lungs. As I'm learning, swim starts are always horrible because there's never a chance to gently warm up, no opportunity to become accustomed to holding one's breath whilst in a state of exertion before going into the state of super -high exertion required to race to the best of one's ability. What's left is the very definite sense that I'm not swimming any faster than normal, but it's causing me a lot more trouble. I know from experience that it can take me around twenty minutes in the water to start moving more freely and rhythmically and at least ten before my breathing settles down.

But today I don't have that kind of time. I've set myself a goal: I want to be in and out within fifteen minutes.

'Yes, you're short of breath but you won't die,' I tell myself. 'Enjoy the water. Doesn't it feel . . . amazing?'

It's only now that I'm noticing it. The water doesn't taste salty like in the Caribbean, nor is it murky and mouldy like in Lanzarote. There's a cool freshness to this lake which is delicious on the tongue (and up the nose, down the throat and, inevitably, in the stomach) and certainly makes the effort required during those first few body-shocking minutes quite literally more palatable.

Everything and nothing runs through my mind during the next 750 metres. There are blissful stretches of silence as well as thoughts of the task at hand – about the placement of my arms and how they mustn't cross over in front of my head, creating unhelpful resistance in the water. I think about transition, grateful that Bella remembered the wristband, and then worry that I won't find my bike in those rows of wheels, shoes and helmets.

I dart between future and past. I think about Ren and wonder, with dread, where in the crowd she'll be hiding, and then I wonder, fleetingly, what the rest of the summer holds. I also think about how far I've come since that first swim in the Grenadines, with Becky Adlington's swim cap and the four safety boats. For a second there is a flickering of pride, as I think not just of my own achievements but of all the women who, like me, have taken a journey via triathlon, facing their fears, limitations and frustrations.

Once I'm out of the water, the game is really on. I trudge up the ramp and onto the long carpet that marks three hundred metres of dizzying, barefoot, sodden running. I'm slogging along fairly slowly, trying to yank down the cord from behind my back so that I can rip off the top half of my wetsuit, when I hear an Irish voice from the crowd.

'Fry! Stop farting around and attack transition!'

For a few seconds I forget the unpleasant burning sensation around my neck where the wetsuit has rubbed and look around.

'Hey! Ren!' I yell, grinning and waving madly, much like a child who has just seen their parent on the sidelines of school sports day.

Except this parent, it turns out, is not best pleased.

'Don't look at me for fuck's sake!' I hear, through my water-clogged ears. 'Get on with it!'

My legs begin to move faster and soon I feel the change from plastic to grass beneath my feet. I have entered the transition zone. Now to rip this damn thing off. It's like Lanzarote all over again: the wetsuit legs get twisted, I try to step on them but end up sitting down and pulling them any which way until I'm free. This time I don't bother with a towel and I've had the foresight to leave my cycling shoes undone and open so it's easy to step in. Helmet on before I lay a finger on my bike. I run my bike along the grass with me until – yes – I hit the concrete, go over the little red mat, hear my timing chip beep to mark the start of the ride, pop one foot on a pedal and clip my cleated shoe in. The other foot on the other pedal – clip – and I'm off.

The cycle course involves three laps of the main road through the park, and is 22.5 kilometres in total. It's warm but not hot; the course is almost flat, with one noticeable but gradual incline between Hyde Park Corner and Kensington, a few speed bumps that bring me out of my seat (to save my joints) and two 180-degree bends that require slowing down to a crawl.

Compared to Lanzarote? It is a walk – a ride – in the park. The fact that the course is easier, however, merely allows me to go faster. The end result in any triathlon should arguably be the same – did you do your best and go as hard as you could? Along the mostly flat stretches of this park, my legs are certainly making their displeasure known. It takes quite a few minutes to get used to this heat in my thighs, and for my body to realise that today my mind is in charge. On the second of the very tight bends I see Dad, bedecked in a bright orange baseball cap and safari-style jacket, camera dangling from one shoulder. I think, with amusement, how pleased I am that we don't share a sense of fashion, and for a moment I feel completely over-whelmed by emotion. My father and I, for many years, had a rather hit-and-miss and at times distinctly difficult relationship, which has been very painful for both of us. Over the last few years we've worked hard, both individu-ally and together, to heal. I think to myself now, mid-pedal stroke, how it is as if we've been given a second chance, an opportunity to rebuild. My father is taking that chance now, coming here, standing about for over an hour, staring out at cyclist after cyclist, hoping one of them will be his daughter and that he can get behind the lens and – click – take one good picture.

How many other families are here today? I wonder. How many other cracked relationships being mended by way of offering support around corners and by the water's edge?

'Hi, Dad!' I yell out to him, taking one hand off the handlebars to wave.

Stop farting around! says Ren's voice inside my head.

But this time I ignore it, continuing to slow down around the corner until I know I've caught my father's eye.

Gratefully, I see it. It's there in his face, clear – clearer than I've ever seen it, perhaps. He is proud, very proud, of his little girl, and for a minute or so I'm four years old again, Dad's hand on the back of my saddle, stabilisers off and bicycle wobbling precariously from side to side as he pushes me forward with encouraging shouts.

I come out of the corner, and the time for reminiscences has passed. Back to the present and the matter in hand. I think about shifting down a gear and playing it safe, but no. Not today, not yet. I came here with an intention – to really and truly test myself – and this is the moment I get tested. One lap becomes two. Two laps moves into three until, halfway round this third, I'm relieved to have some fresh focus beyond the revolutions of the pedals. It comes in the form of a Hispanic man whose T-shirt declares him to be Jesus. Jesus and I play cat and mouse for the entire duration of the third and final lap of the ride: he's ahead until he drops his speed to take a drink; then I get ahead. I'm there, pulling away, until, wait . . . I've pushed it too hard on a small incline and now Jesus, who has managed his cadence and gearing better, is in front again.

And so it goes on, over and over. I don't even know if he notices, but in my head we are racing. Except – damn Jesus! – he's approaching the dismount line ahead of me, but then thankfully he steps off his bike a full three feet or so before the line, allowing me to slip past and dismount right next to it, with centimetres between myself and potential disqualification. It's a small thrill, but to be savoured nonetheless. If there's one dude we generally accept we can't get the better of in life, it's Jesus, after all.

I come back into transition, rack my bike, take my helmet off and change my shoes.

At last, it's time to run. That rather gruesome emptiness is there in my legs, as expected. But either it's not as bad as I remember it or I'm plain stronger. The first lap begins and very shortly after I've got going, I spot Bella in the crowd. She is screaming my name whilst holding a beautiful nine-month-old baby with exquisitely chubby arms and a Mohican quiff of strawberry blonde hair.

Is that ours? I almost think, in a moment of fatigue-induced delusion, remembering quickly that the baby – Evelyn – belongs to one of two female friends who have come to support. They reveal themselves as I pass, just alongside Bella, all three women whooping and hollering their support.

Standing next to them and a little to one side is Ren.

'Don't stop don't stop don't stop,' I think.

But I can't resist pausing momentarily to deposit a kiss on the little babe's cheek.

'Focus and commit!' yells Ren, appalled at my momentary hiatus.

I continue, amused and uplifted, hearing the clatter of plastic beneath my feet as I head down a gangplank and onto a straight road full of other runners.

'I totally forgot how nasty this bit feels,' I say, almost happily, to another competitor.

'You're looking strong,' he says, although it's him who's doing the overtaking. 'Besides, you've got some noisy supporters there.'

The chatty man jogs on fast. I can't keep up, and watch the ground pass beneath my feet, every step a step closer to the start of the next lap and another glimpse of my support crew.

Time does funny things to runners. Especially hapless,

knackered runners. I feel as if it's been hours – days even – since I saw them last and yet I also know it's been around ten minutes. Finally, and in no time at all, I spot Bella again. She's in exactly the same position, only this time she's given the baby back to its rightful owner.

Ren is still there too. 'Go on, Fry, you're doing well, buddy,' she says in a steady tone and with none of the jolliness of my other supporters. It's a compliment of epic proportions from Ren, and one which, given its relative scarcity, fills me with strength to push forward, a little bit faster, faster, faster.

The second lap really, really hurts. I yearn for music now, but personal headsets, and the way they shut off hearing and consequential awareness, are deemed a potential hazard and not allowed. I'm pretty sure that, being a person of a very auditory bent, if I was allowed the help of my chosen music I'd knock at least a minute off my time. But today I'll have to make do with visual markers. I see a man who, years of running have enabled me to estimate, must be going at about seven and a half minutes per mile.

That's about half a minute per mile faster than I'd usually run, on a good day.

One part of me wants to catch him.

The other tells me no. *What's the point? You don't need to. You're so, so tired.*

Which one is me? Or perhaps the most important question is: which is more me, right at this very moment? And – even more important still – which one will win?

The answer is in my proud, ambitious legs: not only do I catch him up, but I pass him and forge onwards. I see pieces of the park I recognise from the first lap – a curve here, a skewed pavement there, and a little bridge that looks down onto Buckingham Palace – each of them signalling to my body that I'm making progress, I'm nearly there, it's nearly over, the end's in sight. But I never see either man, my temporary pacemaker or Jesus, again.

I approach the final straight, vaguely aware of the sound of my feet hitting the ground.

From the stands I hear Ren yell out, 'Come on, Fry! Work harder!'

I think I speed up; I certainly try. Here comes the end. The victorious raising of the arms, hands aloft, as I cross the line.

Slump. Wheeze. Medal. Water. Grin. My legs seize up immediately and my skin feels filthy, covered in sweat and dirt, my mouth and fingers still tacky from ripping open and sucking down an energy gel. But none of that matters one bit; I feel less frustrated than in St Lucia, more proud of my performance than in Lanzarote.

'Well done, Fry. You bossed it,' says Ren, when we're reunited.

It means a lot to hear that from her. But even this unqualified congratulation from Ren is usurped by what happens next, as I grab Bella and pull her into a tight (and, for her, almost certainly quite unpleasant) hug.

'I'm so proud of you,' she whispers into my ear. 'And being here, watching everyone, I feel so inspired.'

'I know,' I reply. 'It's actually quite awesome, isn't it?'

'It is,' she says, lovingly pushing me back before she becomes completely sodden with my sweat. 'I think I want to do one . . .'

I frown, wondering if my battered body and befuddled brain are playing tricks on me.

'What?' I ask. 'You want to –'

'Yes. I want to do a triathlon.'

13

Three down, three more to go. Five days later, on the eve of my fourth triathlon, Bella and I drive to the beautiful English village of Woodstock. We've chosen to make a mini-break of it and stay the preceding night rather than wake at 5 a.m. to travel here from London in time for the triathlon. It's a surprisingly nostalgic affair. We take a walk around our old university town of Oxford, amusing ourselves and each other with stories about who did what where and wondering again how it was that we never managed to meet during the two years we crossed over as students there.

The last time I was in the Blenheim Palace grounds was over a decade ago. It was my third year – the big one – and to stave off the stress of revising for our final exams a group of friends and I established the Pub Grub Club. After making one another mocking, individualised membership cards, we headed off on the first of our club outings to Woodstock for a Sunday roast and an ale in a low-beamed haven nearby, after which we took our hangovers for a walk in Blenheim Palace gardens.

How much has changed since that day, I reflect. I look back upon my twenty-one-year-old self and feel a mixture of affection and embarrassment. She was so self-assured, so entitled, yet so uncertain and so desperate; in a constant state of war with herself. Thankfully it's mostly a different

– better – world I live in today, seen through different – brighter – eyes, and I'm relieved that my younger self, replete with all that fear, translucent confidence and obvious inexperience, doesn't have to tackle tomorrow's triathlon.

But neither the sobriety of age nor the fact that I've done sprint-distance events like today's twice before now seem to eradicate the anxiety that gathers around me like a moth-eaten coat. What I have learned, however, is that the best way of approaching the inevitable self-doubt that immediately precedes a race is to name it: nerves. Yes, that's right. Those gnatty voices that tell you you don't belong here; you were pressured into it; you have a sniffle; your cat will get lonely at home; you can't swim, bike or run; you're just not this kind of person . . . It's hard to believe it at the time but, really, those are just nerves. They are powerful too, able to take over your body, drain your energy, create phantom sicknesses and turn your mind into sticky mud. But whatever they tell you, they really are *just nerves.*

The best thing to do with them is to accept and acknowledge, accept and acknowledge, accept and acknowledge, over and over, without doing anything more drastic than breathing. As long as you don't let them beat you, you're already winning. It helps, I've found, to remember that you're not the first person to stand at the beginning of a triathlon, or lie awake the night before, and wonder what on earth you've got yourself into. Nor will you be the last person to cross the finish line having bitched and moaned to your mates for weeks on end about what a pointless hassle it all is and then almost immediately blabber on about the next one you plan to do.

When I wake up the following morning there are other concerns to add to the usual mix of excitement, curiosity and nerves. Because, as revealed by a quick twitch of the curtains, yesterday's portentous weather forecast was, in fact, spot on.

Storms, heavy rain, hail and – as if that wasn't enough – *flash floods.*

I had tried to ignore it; they get it wrong, sometimes, don't they?

'This isn't ideal,' I say, crawling back into bed next to where Bella lies all warm and snoozy.

Maybe if I close my eyes and wait, I'll realise it's a bad dream?

Maybe not; the noise made by cars driving past on the road below is indisputable – the swishing sound of displaced water. Lots and lots of water.

The course will be a washout. Swimming in heavy rain is probably fine, although if there's the slightest sniff of lightning most triathlon organisers will cancel the swim part if not all of the event. But I've been warned by Suzanne, who has done this event before, that there's a steep hill leading up and out of the swim ('a great place to overtake people if you have the energy', she writes), which presumably in bare feet, when muddy, isn't brilliant. The run will be wet and a little slippery, I guess, but the ride? Cycling in these conditions won't just be horrible, it could also be dangerous.

I make a cup of instant coffee and try not to panic.

'Pity the poor spectator,' Bella mumbles, beginning to wake up.

'Maybe next time it'll be you,' I say.

'Maybe,' she says. 'I need to enter one, don't I?'

As we drive into the palace grounds a few hours later, it's not looking good. Drenched marshals and demoralised competitors slip about in the mud underneath an apocalyptic sky. But around midday the weather turns on its head. Sodden triathletes who have already completed their race stare up at the sky in confusion, while those who like me have yet to start begin to grin.

I shoot Bella a wink goodbye and make my way down a grassy hill along with another sixty or so women who are about to start in our female-only wave. By 1.30 p.m., when, after a few minutes' treading water, I hear the starting horn, it is the best British summer weather that any triathlete could hope for. I've been so busy worrying about the storm that I haven't really had time to get nervous – more plain pissed off – so I'm hungry to get going, and for the first time I actually take Ren's advice about starting at the front of the swim.

Don't let all those other bitches get in your way.

A momentary smile, just before I put my head down and go, as I hear that growling Irish voice inside my head. The water is murky but delicious; I can taste its freshness, just as I can sense my own increased confidence in it. Last weekend has changed things for me. I've been emboldened by what, I discovered afterwards, was actually a rather decent performance for a beginner triathlete: fourteen minutes and fifty-nine seconds for the 750-metre swim, forty-three minutes and twenty-seven seconds for the 22.5-kilometre cycle, and twenty-two minutes and seven seconds for the five-kilometre run. I had merely looked at the numbers on the results page, the time it took for each individual portion of the race (first transition, an unimpressive four minutes and forty-four seconds; second transition, two minutes thirty-six), and missed one particular number that many triathletes consider most important of all – the age-group ranking.

It was Jane Egan, in fact, who, after receiving a blissed-out, endorphin-tastic message from me to say I'd finished, congratulated me on coming nineteenth in my age group (30–34).

Nineteenth? Out of twenty or two thousand? That was surely the question.

Nineteenth out of 105, was the answer. I also placed fifty-sixth out of the 440 women and four hundred and forty-third out of the total of 1370 men and women who finished the sprint distance.

Today the swim is the only part that's exactly the same as last week, the only part where I can directly compare my performance, and while I was happy to have snuck in just under fifteen minutes for 750 metres six days ago, I'm determined this week to do better. I make a conscious decision to try and take fewer strokes, be more relaxed and, instead of letting my legs float behind me as a wetsuit conveniently allows, to use them, just a little, just enough to help me flutter forwards faster without tiring them before the ride.

About halfway through, I have the odd feeling that I am working with, rather than against, the water. My breathing is laboured, certainly, but I'm not half suffocating. I'm reaching forward, stretching out and making an S-shape with my forearm as I use the large muscles on the side of my back to pull my entire body ahead.

I'm swimming quite well, I think, trying to contain my excitement so as not to allow it to jeopardise anything.

Just then I'm joined by another woman who, despite the enormous amounts of space to her left, has decided to swim as close to me as humanly possible.

Her hand keeps catching my foot.

Is she . . . could she be . . . drafting? It's allowed during the swim, but it's both distracting and annoying, that's for sure.

Don't let those bitches . . .

Yes, there it is again. Ren's voice. Just when I need it. I stay my course. Let my arms come out a little to the side just in case this drafting lady needs reminding who's in the lead.

As I'll later discover, it's fourteen minutes and two seconds after beginning that I exit the water and, although during the entire event there are far faster female swim times than mine, in this particular wave I'm amongst the first ten to clamber out and up the ramp. What's most important to me is that I'm a full six minutes faster than I was in St Lucia. Granted, that was a 'no wetsuit' swim, which makes one less buoyant and thus most likely slower (though the salt in the Caribbean Sea might have redressed that), but still I'm absolutely ecstatic with that result.

Transition, again, isn't my strongest suit. Part of the issue is the extreme dizziness that I feel for the first few minutes after the swim. I notice, when I arrive after a two-minute uphill run, that the woman who has racked her bike next to mine has an entire storage box full of stuff. It's packed so neatly that I can only imagine it's organised in order that the things she will require in the first transition are on top and those for the second are underneath.

'This really is a whole new level of obsessive organisation,' I think.

Then again, being fast and flawless – as opposed to slow and clumsy – in both transitions probably takes a minute or two off an overall race time, and what's more, in terms of energy expenditure it's 'free' – a lot easier than finishing both the ride and the run a minute quicker. I ask myself: am I missing something here? Should I be spending time in my house, jumping into the bath in my wetsuit, rushing downstairs to my bicycle to rip off my wetsuit, dry myself and head out onto the road for a ride, over and over again, until I've cracked it?

Probably I should. But, being honest, I'm beginning to think that transition, in triathlon, is what separates the women from the weirdos. Women like me and Ren, who told me that she holds the record in her tri club for the longest/worst ever T1 (from swim to bike), tend to focus on the training and effort, rather than packing labelled garments and drinks into boxes that are then placed in the way of neighbours' transition areas. I have my quirks, I decide, but I've never been a 'practical' person. I'm notoriously bad at performing common-sense tasks, particularly under pressure. Perhaps I simply need to accept that I'm a woman and not a weirdo. After all, isn't this the whole point? I'm trying to find peace with my limitations. And yet old habits die hard. Right now, in this race, just as last weekend at Hyde Park, I have the same thought: I wish I'd been faster, slicker, more compulsively organised – and well-practised – about this. I wish I were more weirdo.

One small consolation today is that I get cracking with hard cycling as soon as my feet clip into those pedals. Still breathless from transition, I force myself to push from the get-go, whizzing past a couple of women who are starting out gently. The course, as Suzanne has rightly informed me, is 'lumpy rather than hilly', but in any case the lumps are noticeable, and one in particular is more like a mound. At least the downhill part offers a chance to freewheel and in-hale much-needed oxygen, plus the mini-lakes (at the bottom of the 'lumps') that one competitor warned me of ear-lier are already showing signs of drying out.

The ride is three laps of the road that runs through and around the two-thousand-acre grounds of Blenheim Palace – 19.5 kilometres in total.

'Take the first lap easy and see what the course is like,' advised that same man who told me about the mini-lakes. 'Then crank it up on the second, and go harder on the third.'

I do nothing of the sort. Instead, I take it hard on the first, harder on the second, and even harder on the third. There are a couple of ladies against whom I appear to be actually 'racing', confirmed by the fact that we go back and forth passing one another, and also by a group of lads who shout out, 'Go on, girls! This is like a real peloton!' But other than that, the course is heavily inhabited by women who seem to have absolutely no idea about the rules of riding. Instead of remaining a suitable distance behind one another and pulling out only to overtake, they frequently cycle alongside each other, leaving very little space for me, and the aggressive, ambitious triathlete I have become, to pass.

A few months ago I'm sure this wouldn't have really bothered me. But I learned a lot about cycling in Lanzarote and today I'm infuriated by the hold-up.

'On your right!' I yell, indicating for the slower ladies to move to the left so that I can squeeze by.

More than anything, it's a safety call – a warning, deliberately loud and brazen enough to reduce the likelihood of a crash – but still, as I scream out, I'm hit with a memory of an organised bike–run event I did around eight years ago, where a male rider nearly sliced my arm off as he powered past angrily, yelling exactly those same three words ('On your right!'). At the time I felt confused by his behaviour and muttered something about how *this is supposed to be fun! Why must you take it all so seriously?*

But people change. And triathlon has changed me. I'm on your right. Get out of my way. Because every second counts.

───────

Sadly my mammoth effort doesn't really translate, as I feel it should, into a mammoth ride. So focused am I on getting ahead in the cycle that it's not until the last kilometre I realise I've made what might soon prove to be a fairly significant error: I haven't switched gear cogs for the entire ride. This means I've been using the top ten gears, meant for faster, flatter cycling, for nearly twenty kilometres, which is an expensive way of using energy, only without serious consequence if your thighs are supremely conditioned.

'Be careful,' Suzanne had warned. 'When I did Blenheim Triathlon I foolishly decided to ride up every lump at max effort to test my fitness. I killed my legs so had zip left in them for the run, whoops!'

Whoops indeed. As always, I have to learn the hardest way. The moment my running shoes hit the deck, I feel it happen: dead legs. A hunched back. Yes – triathlon is a finely tuned balancing act of pushing forward and holding back, requiring a humble appreciation of one's own limits as much as a few risky attempts to break right through them. Have I overcooked it on the ride? And will this recent mistake now prove impossible to recover from?

I can't go back in time now. I have no choice but to continue with these legs, these lungs, this bright yellow Jungle Biking top that I bought back in St Lucia.

'Go Jungle!' yell a few friendly spectators as I loaf down the first straight of the run, the breathtaking baroque architecture of the palace looming over me from behind.

The supporters' amusement makes me smile, just a little, just enough. I snarf a gel and start to plan: *you can have five minutes of easy-ish running,* I promise Exhausted Self. *After that you'll feel differently, something will kick in, I know it will. I'll look after you, or else . . . or else you'll just have to pull something out the bag, OK?*

OK, Exhausted Self replies. *You're the boss.*

About one and a half kilometres later, 'something' still hasn't kicked in. I'm shattered and disappointed. Where are the legs I ran with last weekend? What's happened to them?

I want them back. I want them here. And I want them now! I look for signs, helpful overheard phrases or favoured epithets. I need anything – something – to speed me up, to help me find last weekend's legs. A female runner flies by, going at double the pace of the rest of us, but she is so far out of my league that I find it demoralising rather than energising. I try to yell words of encouragement to the very slow, and to look around me once in a while and take in the luscious green park. I even try an old trick to kid my body into believing it's full of beans, by bouncing up the hills on the balls of my feet.

None of it is working.

Two kilometres. Two and a half . . . The course is replete with spectators, particularly now it's a clement twenty-three degrees and sunny, but their faces meld into an impersonal blur. I haven't seen Bella since the final lap of the cycle ride. The total run is 5.7 kilometres (unlike last weekend's five), and I'm nearing the three-kilometre mark now. I feel unsatisfied. I don't want to go home tonight having petered out at the end of the triathlon in this way. I need something, someone –

'You should be going faster,' says a brawny bloke in a long-sleeved cream T-shirt, looking me up and down as I come by.

He is standing there with a cool drink in one hand and a mullet hairstyle on his head.

I am too shocked, momentarily, to reply, but it's got me riled. By the time I think of something (unrepeatable) to say, I've passed out of earshot.

Should?

My brain buzzes with doubt.

Should be going faster?

Should I?

If I should, then surely I could?

I look for other reasons why he might have said this, ticking them off as possibles one by one:

- I am going far slower than I think.
- Mullet Man is trying to help bolster me.
- Mullet Man thinks I look too athletic to be going so slowly (my personal favourite).
- Mullet Man is, quite simply, an asshole.

Well, Mullet Man can fuck right off, I think indignantly, and find another gear. Why or where that gear has been hiding thus far I honestly don't know, but I don't need a timer to tell me that the last two and a half kilometres are probably around a minute per kilometre faster than those preceding them. A final push up the last hill and I overtake a woman who has been racing along within my sights, yet unreachable, for almost the entire race.

Take *that*, Mullet Man, I think.

I want to find him but he is nowhere to be seen. I charge on and finish the job with another surge, crossing the line, lips sticky with dehydration, body burning and broken from that final effort.

'What was my time?' I say to a nearby race official.

He looks up at the clock. 'One hour, thirty-one minutes, seventeen seconds,' he says.

My shoulders drop and I smile; this is serious progress.

It's almost exactly the same time as in St Lucia, but for a significantly longer, arguably tougher course, and much more time-consuming transitions too. Triathlon delivers on its promise that if you work hard and train consistently then, provided you are able to push yourself in race conditions, you will be astounded by the results. What would happen, I wonder, if I took a longer-term view, as Rob suggests? What could I do? What couldn't I do? New doors open, new possibilities arise.

There's one area, however, where doors are closing rather than opening. The question of financial cost is becoming increasingly problematic. In the week after the Blenheim race I face some rather dull but indubitable truths: I cannot afford to do everything I had planned. There should be two and a half months between now and my final event, the Olympic-distance triathlon in Chantilly. I get to work on researching accommodation and transport costs – I will need to hire a car if we are to take the bike and necessary gear – not to mention other expenses like food and drink. Since this event is scheduled for the final UK summer bank holiday weekend, prices are higher than normal for ferries and hotels. I've already torched my bank account with the trip to Lanzarote, and the predicted amount for a triathlon in France begins to mount up, in a major way. I can hardly believe my own calculator, but numbers don't lie: for Bella and I to go together we're looking at around £600, minimum.

Should I break the bank for an experience that could be

memorable, or should I go back to the drawing board and pick a new event slightly closer to home? Time to change the game plan, I decide, and I begin to scour race listings online. After a few minutes I stumble across one that catches my eye: the first ever Newcastle Triathlon. It looks like an iconic course, starting with a swim in the River Tyne, followed by a ride and run in and around the city. I have a gut feeling that this could be the one, but there is a fairly big catch: it is taking place on 19 July, just five weeks away. Will I have enough time, I wonder, to prepare myself for the full Olympic distance? I had planned to take around nine weeks to build up distances in training, with the hope that I could well and truly improve upon my previous Olympic-distance performance.

The first thing I do is speak to Paula, with whom I've agreed to race in France in August. Since we last met in January she has moved up to Edinburgh. She's been so busy finding her feet in Scotland, she explained, that she hasn't used them much at all. She has at least been swimming in the city's fifty-metre Commonwealth pool, she tells me, but she knows she'll have to enter something soon to really become invested in training again. She can't find the motivation without an event on the horizon.

I apologise again that our proposed race has been compromised by finances but she understands and we agree to give up on our original plan. I ask her if she is free to do the Newcastle event with me instead, but she has a pre-existing engagement in London on 19 July. We run through a few different options but it is impossible to find a suitable and affordable triathlon that works for both our schedules.

'Maybe we'll both end up in St Lucia again next year for the triathlon,' I say, feeling disappointed that we couldn't make any Plan B work.

'Yes,' she laughs. 'But if we do we'd better do the full distance this time.'

Damned right. But for now I have a more pressing full-distance triathlon to organise. I don't hesitate much, committing the next day to racing in five weeks' time. Fresh possibilities present themselves. I ask Bella if she will join me on the trip – we can make a weekend of it – and she agrees. The cost of transport and accommodation remains a factor, but it is significantly less, and I am determined to complete my year in triathlon within the timeframe.

Newcastle is on. Newcastle is mine. And now I've got some serious training to do.

14

Later in the month, two things happen that halt my progress. Firstly I discover, not more than a couple of weeks
after entering, that the Newcastle event is being relocated.
The organisers are distraught; they have spent around two
years working to bring the inaugural triathlon to their city,
and with little more than a month to go they have been
informed by the Port of Tyne Authority that permission
to hold the event has been rescinded. Why? Surely it is not
just because – as my cousin's husband, who grew up near
Newcastle, proudly informed me – revellers urinate in the
river every Friday night on their way back from the pub?
After all, as every triathlete knows, that's the first thing to
happen inside one's wetsuit as soon as one gets knee-deep
in the water. (It's warming, but moreover it's the last opportunity to pee for a few hours.) When I enquire directly, the
organisers tell me that a training exercise, which had nothing to do with them but took place in the Tyne, went awry
and as a result the river was deemed unsafe. Thus, at very
short notice, and with lots of work from those in charge
of the event, the Newcastle Triathlon will now be taking
place around fourteen miles north of the city in Ashington's
Queen Elizabeth II Country Park, in the grounds of the
Woodhorn Museum. And entrants who don't like it? They
can get a full refund.

No refund for me. While I'm a little sad not to be freestyling it down the river, or transitioning along the Quayside, I'm still going ahead with this event, wherever the hell it ends up being. What's more worrying is that I've lost my mojo. For two days after the Blenheim event I felt tired and low but put it down to post-race fatigue. The thing is, it hasn't fully lifted since – I go swimming but I feel unmotivated, slow and almost the same as I did in January. Despite fantastic summer weather, I can't be bothered to actually take my bike out on the roads or to the park but instead just do the odd turbo session at home in our back garden. When I head out for runs, I feel tired. Even in yoga classes I can't tune in with any kind of focus. I know that improving at cycling – probably my weakest area and yet the most dominant discipline in triathlon – in particular is all about miles covered, and hours spent, on the bike. But I just can't, or won't, do it.

I need to find energy and verve, and I need to do it fast, so I start dialling, typing and texting. It's time to ask the triathlon world for help.

Everyone agrees that after an intense period of focus, there can be a fallout. 'You are on a major high after finishing a race and then you come down, as you have hit a climax and now you're out the other side,' says Ren. Her advice? 'Try to get focused on your next race, and you'll find your mojo again.' Rob, as always, takes a longer-term and more philosophical view. 'I am not too surprised that you feel a little burnt out,' he writes. 'It has been an intense and full-on experience. You need and deserve a break. If you love it, you will miss it and then come back to it. If you don't miss it, then it was not meant to be, and you will have gained some really valuable experiences and ticked those Bucket List boxes.'

But there will be no breaks until the Newcastle Triathlon box is ticked. Rob suggests we do an exercise he commonly does with other clients: the Why Game. Remind yourself why you are doing this, he urges: what needs are being met by this particular event?

'Find those reasons, unique to you, which give you images, phrases, memories – whatever – to hold on to while you go through another tough challenge,' he says. 'Then go out there and rejoice in your incredible physical fitness that sustains you through it all, in your impressive mental discipline that doesn't let you quit, and in your good fortune to live a life that affords you all these opportunities to do super-cool stuff like triathlon.'

I get to work writing down my reasons for this entire triathlon challenge, and in particular, for heading up to Newcastle in a few weeks to tri once again:

I set myself a task – a year in triathlon, and to understand the appeal – and I will complete that task.

I know I'll feel an amazing sense of achievement afterwards.

I am committed to getting stronger and overcoming obstacles without beating myself up too much in the process.

I am a person in transition, as well as a triathlete in the making. This is an educational process, all about progress, and not perfection.

I am doing this, quite simply, because . . . why not? Because I can. I will continue to tri for the people who, for whatever reason, want to but just can't.

Next I write down some phrases I've made up or picked up along the way:

Tough times don't last; tough people do.
Go hard or go home.
Life begins on the edge of your comfort zone.
Never, ever give up.
Pain is temporary. Pride is forever.

There's more too – everybody in the tri world has their own toolkit of mental images, videotapes and phrases which they are happy to share. One triathlete friend, Laura, tells me she likes to imagine the commentary that surrounds her race: 'She's working so hard, but can she maintain excellent composure? Can she get that all-important podium position today?' Another runner friend of mine who enters the occasional triathlon event tells me her mantra is: 'Do not stop, think of the cake, do not stop, think of the cake.' Emily tells me that her bike bears words written on it by Chrissie Wellington herself, the same words record-breaking swimmer Diana Nyad often uses: 'Never, ever give up.' Whatever works. We find our way through the pain. Whether healthy or unhealthy, we find our motivation and our saving graces and we use them to our advantage.

I write down a few more ideas or words that I might call upon in three weeks' time, during the Newcastle Triathlon:

It's just three hours of your whole life.

This is your choice. You brought yourself to this place.

In the end, it is only a triathlon. It doesn't really, really matter.

You are enough, just as you are.

And the one which always makes me smile – Rob's words to me (and most probably to all the triathletes in his care) before the Volcano Triathlon in Lanzarote:

You are awesome. You have always been awesome. And you will always be awesome.

All of this helps, but not enough. What really turns the tide is what I witness one perfect summer's evening in early July at Hever Castle in Kent. In the immediate high after the Blenheim race, I had planned to take part in this extra-special sprint-distance event. I was partially drawn by the timing, a Wednesday evening being an unusual time to hold a triathlon, but also the surroundings. After all, I'd just knocked off a race in a palace. Why not try a castle next?

When the day comes, though, I decide to stand on the sidelines instead. My misplaced verve has meant not only lost training hours but also lost confidence. I've considered ditching the entire trip, using a sore right shin as a (not entirely invalid) excuse. I've never been one for half measures, but I'm persuaded by the event's marketing queen, Yvonne, that an uncharacteristic compromise is a good approach.

'I'm sure it'll help if you just come and see what the Castle Tri is all about,' she says as we drive from the parochial Kent station where she's picked me up down windy lanes to Hever Castle. 'I think what we do is really special. It's all about inclusion and friendliness. The first adult wave starts at 6.30 p.m. but the kiddies start an hour before.'

'Kids?' I ask.

'Oh yes, they totally love it,' she says. 'They just rock up after school and race!'

Yvonne tells me proudly that over 1500 children took part in the 2013 Hever Castle weekend event that completes the annual Castle Triathlon series. Tonight, there will be around 150 aged between eight and fifteen, going off in age-group waves that span two years. I feel a little perturbed. Children? Doing a triathlon? Is that really a good idea? I know what strain it places on the body, after all. Yet the distances for the youngsters are short, the smallest being a hundred-metre swim, four-kilometre ride and 1.3-kilometre run for the eight-to-ten-year-olds. But – here's a question – do they really have a choice in the matter, or is it more the insistence of their triathlon-obsessed parents that they take part?

It is not only the health hazards of triathlon for young children that preoccupy me but also something less altruistic. I can feel pinpricks of jealousy ripple across my skin. There's something irking me here about lost opportunities and gender dynamics. If triathlon had been more available when I was young, might I have taken to it? As a young girl, I adored football and cricket, watching both avidly on television as well as playing them at every opportunity. I remember summer holidays aged seven or eight, hours spent with a bat and ball in the garden whilst my long-suffering big brother entertained and coached me. Gradually, my technique improved. If catching, I watched the ball right into my hands, just as he instructed. When standing at the crease, I stepped forward and watched that same ball onto my bat. I knew, by the age of nine, that I preferred the danger and responsibility of fielding at silly mid-off rather than staying out in the deep. I could bowl leg spin, off spin and a googly (though probably not to any remarkable standard) before I was eight. My primary school was hot on gender equality, and girls and boys played all sports together. But then I turned eleven and went to an all-girls secondary school which didn't offer either cricket or football because, I assume, both were still regarded as boys' sports. And that, as they say, was that. I liked hockey, hated netball, and never did much with either.

But tonight at the Hever Castle Evening Triathlon there are as many girls as boys. I hover on dry land whilst the eleven-to-thirteen-year-olds dunk into the water ready to start. Behind me, the eight-to-ten-year-olds gather without any of the hushed mumblings of anxiety that are so commonplace in grown-up events. Unlike adults, where even the most aesthetically pleasing still look as if they have been vacuum-packed in black slime, these youngsters seem to wriggle around in their neoprene as if it were simply a second skin. Their excitement is tangible and infectious too as they jiggle about whilst a nervous parent makes last-minute adjustments to their little darling's kit.

The horn goes and they are off! Kayaks ward the less able swimmers whilst the obvious talents forge ahead. Proud parents push from the sidelines with shouts. When the first child, a boy, exits the water, a huge bunch of us erupt into applause. He shoots through transition at a speed I've only previously witnessed amongst adult professionals. Much to my surprise, every one of these first few competitors step out of the water and onto the gangplank with incredible speed and finesse. As if demonstrating all the positive clichés about childhood, they fly off towards their bicycles with limitless vitality. I think about how much willpower it took recently for me to run, rather than walk, through the first transition at Hyde Park and Blenheim, and wonder: what is it about being a grown-up that makes us so quick to tire and so reluctant to just go for it (and to hell with the consequences)? Certainly there is a longer journey upwards out of the swimming position to standing, and correspondingly greater potential for dizziness and disorientation. We're also heavier, which makes a big difference when it comes to running anywhere but at the same time allows for more power, on the bike in particular. Even the slower and less obviously co-ordinated children who lag far behind the pack still seem to trip off to the next section of their race with an optimism I haven't seen as much of in adult non-elite races. The years pass and, in my experience anyway, we become increasingly encumbered with doubt, negativity and fear. I am more optimistic and joyful now than I have been for at least twenty years but it is still an effort sometimes to remember: none of this shit matters. Embrace the breathlessness and enjoy the speed.

I watch the next few waves come through transition in a similar vein and ask myself whether these children will gain something vital and intangible from these race experiences.

Whilst few of them will make the podiums and win prizes, and most of those are already training regularly, connected with a running or triathlon club, surely it comes at a crucial point in personal development. All of the triathlons I've done thus far have helped me to ditch unhelpful negative beliefs and overcome restrictive fears. They have inflated my sense of self like a hot-air balloon, allowing me to soar over miniature disasters which might previously have knocked me for several days. To be caught by gusts of achievement at such an early age could be very powerful. Life-changing, even. But can these children see it yet?

I wake up the next morning eager to train. Last night has left me frustrated; once the adult races began, to my surprise, I found myself desperate to dive in and rather regretful I had shirked the opportunity to scratch another notch on my triathlon bedpost. So today, after a long outdoor swim in the sunshine – 2600 metres to be exact – I feel a bit like I've been born again. Just in time too, because my next event is now three weeks away. I need to ramp things up, and particularly over the next fortnight, since the week preceding the event will involve a reduced training load so as to keep my body fresh for the big race.

I also need to sort logistics. I was quick off the mark with some things, booking accommodation almost as soon as I switched from France to Newcastle, but have yet to buy our train tickets. The latter is easy enough, and I get it done today, but the former is now causing a problem. The hotel I had chosen, primarily because of its proximity to the Tyne and the original venue of the triathlon, is now not particularly convenient at all if we are to get out to Ashington on the Saturday morning. But staying nearer the triathlon would mean being miles out of town for the remainder of our romantic weekend.

I decide to leave things as they are. Saturday morning could be a mission and there will be walking and buses involved, most probably at some ridiculous hour of the morning, but so be it. Some triathletes do it every other weekend during race season, after all. Besides, these issues can be smoothed out with a little forward planning. The various demands on my wife's time are less easy to navigate. With ten days to go until we leave for Newcastle, Bella takes a deep breath and explains that she has a work commitment which 'might' clash with our weekend away.

She fidgets a little in her seat. Her face is taut as if she's readying herself for an argument. She explains that she has the opportunity to do a three-day course and that the only dates in the foreseeable future that are remotely feasible are those that coincide with my triathlon.

We talk it over for all of five minutes. She is clearly torn.

'Of course you must do it,' I say, interrupting her midflow.

'Really?'

'Yes, really.' I hold her hand. 'I don't want my triathlon stuff to get in the way of you doing anything you want to do.'

Her shoulders drop like a puppet's on a string. It is clear that she was not expecting this reaction and instinctively I'm a little offended. Have I really been so engrossed in triathlon that my own wife is nervous about raising this with me? Triathletes can be selfish, I know. Brutally selfish. To some extent they have to be, particularly when training for the longer-distance events. But not me, I had insisted to myself. I will never be one of those self-involved amateur sportswomen who prance around thinking the world revolves around their training schedule as if they were a professional athlete going for gold.

Oh dear.

I let go of Bella's hand and wonder: have I become that person? If the first two triathlons of my challenge had not taken place abroad, there is no way in hell I'd have let Bella off being there. But something has changed – the whole experience of triathlon has altered my perception of many things. One of them is love. When this project started out, Bella didn't understand its purpose. Or, at least, she couldn't fathom why it had to be leapt into with such intensity. But she supported me nonetheless, listening endlessly to my late-night talk of training and traipsing along to stand for hours on the sidelines of the two recent triathlons at Hyde Park and Blenheim Palace.

Now it's time for me to take a risk. Besides, one thing I've learned during my time as a triathlete is that *I can handle it*. Whatever the challenges that arise, be they getting smacked in the face by a fellow swimmer, cycling up hills in the blazing heat or heading up to Newcastle with my bike on my own for a triathlon, *I am strong enough*.

Bella throws her arms around me. 'Thank you so much,' she says. 'Thank you thank you thank you.'

'You're welcome.'

I smile for approximately three seconds before starting to freak out. Should I go alone to Newcastle then? Yes, I can handle it but I don't want to if I can help it. I'd also like some evidence, at least, that I was there – who will take pictures? I mostly exercise alone (I prefer it, in fact) but I have never turned up to any organised sporting event without back-up. I assume lots of people must do it though, especially if, like me in Newcastle, they don't know anyone else partaking in the event. But they are probably either exceptionally confident or focused solely on improving their race pace. Maybe they are there merely to practise their transitions under race conditions, to see if all that jumping out of the bath in a wetsuit made any difference to their overall finish time.

Whatever. They are weirdos, like the lady with the plastic box in transition at Blenheim Triathlon. Sure, I might have managed to Do the Right Thing just now but let's be clear: I haven't had a complete personality transplant. I still want someone to hold a bag with my protein shake and a jumper for afterwards; someone to whine to before it starts; someone to scream encouragement at me as I crawl out of the water; someone to holler at me as I bob past on the run and to tell me afterwards that it was amazing to watch such athletic elegance in action, that they couldn't believe I didn't win the entire women's race.

I want someone to lie, essentially.

I scrabble around frantically in the drawer of my mental filing cabinet marked *Friends*. There are various criteria that the correct person must fulfil and which force me to discard some people almost immediately.

Must be one of the friends I could imagine spending a chunk of time with, and who could spend a full three days with me.

Must be bribable: free travel and accommodation (perhaps I'd better throw in a dinner too) in return for a long morning's worth of standing around and lying to me about how well I'm doing.

Must be someone who, if there are no more rooms available at the hotel, I am prepared to share a room with. House-trained. Not snorer or insomniac.

And, following on from that last point: *Must be low maintenance and un-neurotic. The kind of person who won't complain about being tired or bored or both.* I can't be worrying about the wellbeing of my supporter when I'm about to do my biggest race.

Must be available in just ten days' time for an entire long weekend. So that discounts anyone with young children, like my sister and brother. It also takes out of the running all those (you know who you are) who book up every single summer weekend with a wedding, festival or Ibizan jaunt.

Very quickly, my mind stops at Emily. No, this isn't tri-athlete Emily, but another one. Part-time cycle courier and part-time writer, this Emily – let's call her Em, that's easier – has thighs of solid rock and curly hair usually tucked under a courier cap. She wears cleated cycling shoes to walk around in, even when she is not getting on her bike, and is more comfortable in trendy courier regalia than any other kind of clothing. She fits all of the above criteria and more. She is effectively a fully trained bike mechanic but also offers excellent companionship and conversation whenever we hang out together. Having cycled solo through Asia – the

Gobi and Taklamakan Deserts, Karakorum Mountains and Qinghai Plateau to be exact – it's unlikely that the small issue of getting up early and standing around, potentially in the rain, is going to faze her. She will most likely enjoy it, especially looking at all the pretty bikes lined up in a row in the transition area.

Keeping absolutely everything crossed that can be crossed, I dial Em's number and ask the question.

To my relief and excitement, she agrees.

I could kiss her right now. I instantly feel more relaxed about the Newcastle trip.

'Wait. Can I bring my bike?' she says.

I think about this. I wonder for a moment why she would need it for a three-day city break up to a place with a perfectly good metro system. But then I remember: where Em goes, her bicycle goes.

'Yeah. Sure,' I say. 'Should be easy enough to sort out another reservation for the train.'

'Brilliant.' Now it's Em's turn to sound relieved. 'And! One more thing . . .'

'Yes?'

This sounds ominous. I ready myself to leap over one last hurdle.

'You're not going to want to talk all the time, are you?' she asks.

I laugh. I understand exactly what she means: *you're not one of those exhausting people who has to fill every silence with some chatter, are you?*

'No,' I say, smiling to myself. 'Are you?'

Within one day it is all sorted. Another hotel room is booked and I reserve a spot on the train for Em's bike. There is just over a week until the triathlon and a suspicious calm descends. I taper my training as instructed by Rob. My work schedule means I cannot follow instructions exactly but I do my final long swim on the Monday and a short bike ride and yoga on Tuesday. I haven't run since the previous Friday but that was a relatively long one – twelve kilometres – and considering my injury history I think it is probably sensible to just leave it now until the race, so no final run on Wednesday.

Without the daily or even twice-daily training sessions, I am left with what feels like a lot of spare time. You might think it would be a relief, enjoyable even, to be under instructions to rest as much as possible but that is not the case in the days before a race. I have more time to feel the now familiar effects of pre-race nervousness, a kind of all-pervasive unease that comes to steal any sense of peace or wellbeing. Normal conversations become difficult; my mind flits between what is being said and what I mustn't forget to pack for the triathlon. My appetite wavers unhelpfully and I find myself quick to become upset about things that might not bother me usually.

Relax, I think. *This is just triathlon. It is a contest for contest's sake.*

It is my new and slightly absurd way of self-soothing. I try to make a fool out of triathlon, reducing it (and, in this

regard, perhaps other solitary sports too) to its basic ten-
ets – a challenge that has emerged in an era when life has,
in some ways and in some places, become so comfortable
and so sedentary as to not be testing enough; people like
me must find a greater, physical challenge with which to fill
their lives with purpose. We swarm together in the water
ready to begin an organised event that will force our bodies
into a state that few of our ancestors would have willingly
entered. Manual labour and war were conditions that neces-
sitated this kind of sustained heart-pumping effort. Triathlon? I suspect they would have marvelled at it. Mocked it
perhaps. Whichever, I find that looking at it this way helps
me remember the element of choice and even the frivolity of
what I'm about to do. I can approach it with a lightness of
touch. Paradoxically, it is this lightness that is required if I'm
to give it everything I have and smash my personal bests for
each discipline into the next stratosphere. Otherwise it gets
too serious. Too heated. The pressure cooker could switch
on. And that would not be good right now.

In this strange downtime before my final race I decide to
catch up on where my triathlon friends are with their own
journeys. First, Ren. There was talk back in May of potential
events in August and September. What is she doing, if anything, about triathlon?

'I was feeling too guilty about all the missed tri club sessions so I've officially taken this season off,' she says. 'I'm just
doing CrossFit this year instead.'

I smile at the use of 'just'. Six times a week, at 6 a.m.,
Ren leaves her house to cycle three miles to a one-hour intensive workout before cycling back and going to work. On

Saturday mornings the class is followed by what she herself calls a 'brutal' running session at a local track. Call it seven tough workouts a week, combined, almost certainly with a sleep deficit and excessive boozing on Friday and/or Saturday nights. That's got to be fairly exhausting as it is?

'Yeah, but I'm happy not to have to fit the swimming and cycle rides in too. Just for now.'

Will she go back to triathlon? I ask.

'Probably, I reckon, yeah. Some of those iconic races have my name on them.'

Next on my list are Suzanne and Emily. It's not easy to track them down when their every evening is taken up by training but we find a time to meet for lunch near Suzanne's office in central London. When I spot them both I am immediately struck by the physical change in Suzanne since we last met some months ago. She is visibly leaner, her shoulders boldly announcing themselves on either side of her black shift dress, leading down to tight arms and wiry, tense legs. She has become someone who, even in her work clothing and from some distance away, betrays her athleticism. I think I'm sporty-looking – if you get close you can see a few individual muscles – and on a confident day I might even call myself defined in most places, except perhaps the stomach. The same would go for Emily. But Suzanne is on another level; her body speaks a different language.

'You're starting to look like Chrissie Wellington!' I say.

It is only now I've said it that I wonder if this is perhaps overly personal, or if it doesn't sound quite so much like a compliment as I intended. Thankfully, though, there's no harm done. Emily places an arm around her girlfriend in what I can't help feeling is a slightly proprietorial way and Suzanne just laughs.

'Yeah, well, I've given up sugar,' she says with gleaming, sugar-free eyes. 'It's amazing. I've got so much more energy. I don't use gels when I'm training any more. I hardly eat wheat either . . . On Wednesday and Saturday afternoons I might break the rules and have a treat if I really feel I need it, but mostly I just don't want it any more.' And then she drops the bomb. 'Oh, and I'm vegetarian. You knew that, right?'

Ironwoman Suzanne who does nothing with her non-work time but exercise is vegetarian? If I could write down on a piece of paper all my ideas on nutrition and training and how the two can help or hinder one another, then this latest revelation is like simply scrunching up that paper and tossing it in the bin. Muscles rip and protein is the main thing that helps them to rebuild. So how can Suzanne repair the huge amount of ripping in her muscle fibres that the intensive and demanding training regime she follows will inevitably cause without the protein found in high-quality meat? Yes, there is protein in plenty of other foods but how can she have the time or energy to be sure she gets enough?

Today, Suzanne chooses a fairly lightweight salad for lunch.

'Is that all you're having?' I say.

'Yeah, but don't worry. I've got nuts and fruit and stuff at work.'

It's hard to argue given how unbelievably well she looks. I have never seen anyone so enthused by their training, nor met a person who follows a regime like Suzanne's and yet appears so energised.

'What's new?' I ask.

'Well, you know I ran the London Marathon in April,' she begins.

I nod. Yes. I knew that. It took her three hours and forty minutes and she was *disappointed*. I know everything is relative, but that she was aiming for three hours thirty is fairly astounding, since she began four or five years ago as a five-hour-marathon kind of girl. Any sadness Suzanne suffered as a result of being ten minutes over her target time in the marathon was knocked aside by a fantastic performance at the Half Ironman event, EtonMan, in June. Here Suzanne finished third-fastest female and then chose in the aftermath to 'swim down' for two kilometres. Since then the focus has been Ironman Zurich, which takes place on 26 July, just a couple of weeks away.

'I just want to keep knocking on the door and seeing what I'm capable of,' she says. 'Life is just much easier being this fit. Although admittedly the negative can be that it's very time-boxed. But I'm never low on energy, either physically or mentally. Every day I get a kick out of achieving something in my training. Even if it's a one-kilometre recovery swim in the Serpentine before work and the sun is on my back and I'm watching bubbles dance through my fingers . . . What a way to start the day!'

It's like she is on another planet. Planet Ironman:

Monday: 6.30–8 a.m.: swim. Lunchtime: strength & conditioning; gym. After work: 90 minutes on the turbo trainer.

Tuesday: recovery swim first thing. 90 minutes turbo in the evening.

Wednesday: complete rest day if she needs it, although she *may* go for a one-hour run.

Thursday: 6.30–8 a.m.: swim 90 mins. After work: bike 60 mins, strength & conditioning 30 mins, then 60 mins swim.

Friday: 6.30–8 a.m.: swim. After work: cycling of some sort.

Saturday: It's all about the long ride. Five hours perhaps? If it's horrible weather Suzanne might do this indoors, on the turbo trainer.

Sunday: two-hour run.

'Oh, and also this Sunday we have two individual one-mile swims to do,' she adds. 'But if I'm exhausted, I might take the Friday biking session out.'

'I do probably less than a quarter of what you do and I'm constantly having to take sessions out,' I say. 'Just to keep the injuries and exhaustion at bay. I really don't know how you manage it.'

I am half expecting a brash response about setting one's mind to something and just getting on with it. But Suzanne's tone is kind and non-judgemental:

'You must listen to your body,' she says. 'There will be plenty more days. Treat minor injuries like major ones, because that's what they will become if you don't listen . . .'

Listen to your body.

I smile. This is one of those phrases that gets bandied about a lot and almost invariably by those people who, by definition, cannot be listening much to theirs. By its very nature, completing an Ironman event, let alone going for a personal best or trying to beat other competitors, necessitates ignoring bodily feedback in almost every way. It's not just Ironman either. This applies to all triathlon; if I had 'listened' to my body in the last year I would have probably completed the sprint distances in around two and a half hours and the Olympic one in five. But I understand what Suzanne is saying. It's not so much that we should pay attention to the human body's natural propensity for laziness but more that we should get to know our bodies. Learn to understand their signals. The regular ouch-exercising-hurts kind of self-chatter is irrelevant. Listening is subtle. It's about being in tune with oneself on every level. And that takes practice and plenty of training. Suzanne is way ahead of me on that.

But even taking into account the four more years of swims, rides and runs that Suzanne has over me, I'm still a bit wide-eyed at the sheer (wo)man-hours she's putting in. I was sure I had a handle on the insanity of long-distance triathlon but hearing it listed in this way has knocked me off my perch. How come Suzanne isn't always ill? I ask if she gets tired but both she and Emily shake their heads; they have a rule never to begin serious conversations after 10 p.m. and are usually asleep by then in any case. I know from my own experience that being fitter (and not having intense conversations after 10 p.m.) does indeed make regular life easier, just as Suzanne has said, and that it tends to increase energy and quality of life rather than deplete it. But surely there is a sweet spot? At what point does it tip over? Yesterday I might have confidently said 'with Half Ironman and Ironman training', but seeing Suzanne so undeniably happy and well has made me question this. Besides, while what Suzanne fits into a week may be inconceivable to me, it is far from uncommon among those training for long-distance triathlons. Jodie Swallow and Hollie Cradduck, both now deep in preparation for September's Ironman Wales, are placing a similar amount of emphasis on swimming, cycling and running and all those bits inbetween. Jodie's schedule in fact looks even more terrifying, and appears to include *no* rest day. Some weeks she will take one, she says, but some weeks she just doesn't really need it. I suppose that being a Masters student means she can fit in her training without scrimping on sleep, but still, a dissertation and 'the world's hardest' Ironman? Those are two very big projects for one academic year.

'And what about you?' I ask Emily.

Though she works part-time as a sports instructor and her training schedule isn't as full as her girlfriend's, it is still fairly rigorous – by most people's standards extremely intense indeed. She joins Suzanne and the rest of their swim club for the Monday, Thursday and Friday 6.30 a.m. sessions. Yet on those same evenings Emily returns to the water for another ninety minutes. Sometimes on weekends she will run or cycle too and she has recently also become a swim coach.

'I want to be like Colin Hill,' she says.

Is he some kind of famous triathlete?

'He did unsupported swims,' she explains.

'Ah, I see. So,' I say, 'no more triathlon then?'

'Well, we'll be doing the Ironman in Australia this December,' she says. 'But really I want to focus on the swimming. I've been doing triathlons for the last three or four seasons and I've raced in three World Championships and won small races. It's unlikely I'll make the Olympics so this will be as high-level as I'll get. I can go longer distances but frankly if you trudge along for long enough you'll get to the other end. Every Bob, Joe and Mary has done one [an Ironman], though it is of course no mean feat. But I don't see speed on its own as defining the benchmark of what human bodies can achieve. It's a small part of it, but I find resilience more admirable. Long-distance swimmers, especially the cold water ones who don't wear wetsuits and are unsupported, are still in relatively uncharted ground. Only 121 people in the world have managed the ice mile. When I finish the Gibraltar Strait in October I will be the first Chinese [person] who has crossed it. I find events with a high DNF [Did Not Finish] rate more interesting and more challenging.'

And now I'm not sure really what comes over me (there's something here about challenges which makes my mind drift to long-term relationships . . .) but I decide to change tack a little. How are they doing as a couple? I ask, aiming for a casual tone. When we last talked properly in December Suzanne had mentioned that it was a struggle to spend enough time together because of their different training commitments. Is this still the case or have things improved in that department?

Emily suggests it is all going very well and Wednesday night is their date night these days. But here Suzanne objects: what about that time when Emily chose to teach instead, or the other time when—

No, that wasn't what happened, Emily replies, and a muddled explanation ensues. The lunch hour is almost up and our plastic boxes are empty but there's one more question on my mind.

'So, Suzanne – what has changed for you since you started triathlon?' I ask as we are standing up to leave.

Suzanne thinks about it, but not for long. 'It's changed what I think I'm capable of, where I go on holiday, what I eat, what I look like, what I spend my time doing and who I hang around with.'

'So that's . . . basically . . . everything?' I say.

We laugh.

'Yes.' Suzanne nods. 'Pretty much. I guess you could say that triathlon has changed my entire life.'

Thursday. The day before I am due to leave for Newcastle. Two days before the triathlon. As I kneel down beside the rear wheel to pump up the tyre, I spot two huge indentations in the rubber.

Shit.

Is this critical or can I still ride it over the forty-six-kilometre cycle course in Saturday's triathlon? I text cycle courier Em immediately and send a picture of the offending tyre. The years of riding bikes for a living make her the closest thing to a bike mechanic that I've got and I need answers, fast.

Should I be worried about this? I ask.

She replies immediately: *Yep. You should be worried. But*

not too worried. I can easily sort it. Could you send me the specs of the old one and I'll pick you up a replacement tyre and fit it when we get to Newcastle.

Seriously? Can I not get round with this one?

You could maybe. But it could slow you down and also will be far more likely to puncture. Not advisable.

A series of swear words leave my mouth in close succession. I want to check I understand:

So I definitely shouldn't ride it like this? Why I ask again I have no idea.

Like I said, you could. But you'd feel like a bit of an idiot if you ruined your race just because you were too lazy to change it, wouldn't you?

Yes, I reply, because I really, really would. Yet again my total ineptitude when it comes to bike mechanics is haunting me. If I ever do this again, I think, I'm going to sort out everything about the bike. Ride more. Fix tyres and learn how the damned thing actually works. But for now, I have Courier Em to the rescue:

Relax, Fry. Replacing a tyre is no big deal, she tells me. *I'm out delivering now and I'll be passing a bike shop soon. I can fit it for you when we get to Newcastle, OK?*

Yes, thank you so much, I text back, for the first time feeling grateful that it isn't my bike-hating beloved who's accompanying me on the final, most important, event of all.

15

Em and I meet at King's Cross Station the following day. At my behest we rendezvous early, forty-five minutes before our train is due to depart for Newcastle. I'm already flustered when I arrive at the cafe where Em sits, as ever, with a book in one hand and her bicycle nearby. It is about as hot as the average English summer gets; the air is humid and I have at least three layers of sweat trapped between my T-shirt and my back. On top of it all is a huge rucksack bought twelve years ago for a two-month post-university trip around Thailand and Australia. The pack is almost as heavy now, crammed with wetsuit, tri suit, cycling shoes, running shoes, helmet and other gear, as it was for that eight-week adventure.

I have a feeling Em is early out of kindness. She is humouring me and I am grateful.

'I'm sorry if I'm a bit jumpy,' I say. 'If it seems like I'm in a bad mood, it isn't with you. I'm just feeling a little –'

'Ah no, that's fine,' she replies with total sincerity. 'I'm fully expecting you to be in a bad mood for the next . . .' She glances down at her watch. 'Oh, almost twenty-four hours exactly. Just under, perhaps?'

I nod. I've explained that the race starts at 8.15 a.m. tomorrow and it should take approximately three hours, so Em's right. In one day's time, notwithstanding disasters, it should all be over.

What a relief that will be. I consistently remind myself that the build-up is part of the process and I should try to appreciate, if not enjoy, this day before the race as much as the race itself or the aftermath.

I buy a coffee and some water. We sit and chat for fifteen minutes.

'Can we go now?' I ask.

Em looks at her watch. It has been tacitly decided that she is the one in charge today.

'No,' she says. 'It's only half eleven. They probably haven't even put the platform on the board yet.'

Our train is at twelve. What if both of our watches stop working at once? What if we become so immersed in conversation that we forget to leave the cafe? I want so much to be unflappable like Em seems, to be one of those people who can stroll onto a train one minute before it leaves without the merest hint of stress. But really I'm thinking: *Argh! We must go NOW! We have these bikes! I've never taken a bike on a train before. Where does it go? Do they tell you, help you, or leave you to guess which carriage is for your wheels? What about finding your seats?* I didn't realise quite how important getting to the start line of this triathlon was to me until this moment. Despite all my insistences that oh yes, it's just another event and I've done an Olympic-distance triathlon before in Lanzarote – I am in fact totally freaking out.

It is 11.35 a.m.

'Can we go now?' I ask again.

'Not yet,' she repeats. 'We will go and find the platform at quarter to twelve.'

She carries on with her story about the rare but possible

communion between taxi drivers and cyclists. I am trying to listen but barely a word of it goes in. Instead I go through tomorrow's race in my head. I make noises to ensure that Em thinks I'm still following her but instead I consider Ren's advice for tomorrow: *I know it is more than double a sprint but treat it as a sprint and go hard all the way and you'll surprise yourself at how you do.*

How does that work, I wonder: how can you treat an Olympic-distance triathlon as you would an event of half the distance? It is triathlon suicide, surely?

Typical Ren, I think, watching the huge station clock tick tick tick the time.

At last, 11.45 a.m. arrives.

'Right, yes! Let's go,' says Em.

I wake with my alarm at 4.50 a.m. It being late July and Newcastle some three hundred miles further north than London, it is fully light already. After tossing and turning for a couple of hours I must have finally dropped off about one. As I open my eyes I'm aware that I've been dreaming about triathlon, half waking every now and again to the knowledge that yes, it is today and it is soon.

Considering how little decent rest I've had, I'm surprised at how alive I feel. I jump out of bed and push open the hotel curtains with the kind of enthusiasm usually reserved only for adverts or cartoon characters. My skin tingles with anticipation every time I conjure up the start line in my mind.

There is no time to lose. Em and I have to be at a meeting point about five minutes' ride away at 5.30 a.m. sharp if we are to get our bikes loaded and onto the bus that the organisers have booked for a select few to get to Ashington. I am grateful for the alertness that comes immediately upon waking from a terrible night; there is no time required to wake up if one has barely gone into a deep sleep. Now I need to sort out today's nutrition. One bottle is filled with water and placed in the back holder on the bike as I will need to reach it a little less often. The other is filled with water and carbohydrate powder and an electrolyte tablet. I shake it up and place on the front holder.

Take a few sips of the energy drink every fifteen minutes, said Rob in his final email. *Plus an energy gel every half an hour when you're on the bike.*

Every half an hour?

I seem to question every single thing the poor man says.

Yes, he tells me: *you need to get to the run with enough energy in you. Ideally, it would be nice to get about an extra 1000 kcal into your system after the swim and before the run but that's highly unlikely. If you drink a whole bottle of sports drink that might be 200 kcal, and then a gel every 30 min might give you another 300–400 kcal over the 1.5 hours or so that you're cycling. Even pushing the drink and gels aggressively, you are still probably going into the run depleted.*

I had no idea that triathlon might burn quite so many calories. When you break it down, though, it makes sense. For someone of my weight and height, a half-hour fast swim might use anywhere between four hundred and six hundred calories, a ninety-minute hard ride might burn a thousand to fifteen hundred, and a ten-kilometre run between seven hundred and a thousand. That's one very creamy curry – times three. Can't I save it all up for that? Sadly no. If I want to perform I'll need to refuel a little as I go along. During Ironman races competitors often stop in transition for a sandwich or two. That sounds a little healthier, but it's time-consuming and almost certainly unnecessary during an Olympic-distance event. Taking some kind of regular energy on board remains essential, however, and synthetic sugar-laden gels are very convenient. Every half an hour, says Rob. That means I will have taken two gels and had a whole bottle of carbohydrate drink before I even begin to run. Then I'll take another one at the start of the run and another halfway through. That's at least double what I took on board in Lanzarote, not to mention a lot of unnatural stuff in one body. Especially a body under duress. What if I feel sick?

Today, for once in my life, I've decided to follow instructions to the letter. I will take four gels during the course of the race.

So I pack six.

All this preparation takes around fifteen minutes. I gulp the remaining coffee and pour some porridge oats that I have brought from home into a hotel mug and mix them with hot water and protein powder. As I stir it, I'm feeling pretty smug about how organised this is and how much stronger I feel than that morning in the Caribbean before my first triathlon. As I take a few bites, the smugness disappears; it is revolting and I have to force it down, remembering that this is about fuel and function rather than eating for enjoyment.

Nothing would be more detrimental to the race than to be hungry on the start line.

Next I dress in my quick-dry sports bra, tri suit and jumper. I put on my cycle shoes and check over the bag I packed last night. Running shoes and socks, a cycling top, wetsuit, swimming cap and goggles. No wristband needed this time as, unlike in Hyde Park, I am registering when I get to the venue, so I will do all the triathlon admin there.

'I'm getting better at this,' I think.

Three hours to go. I have no idea what the course will look like. I haven't a clue if the bike route is technical, if the run is hilly, or how many people will join me in the lake for the swim. I have looked at the race details on the website but staring at diagrams does little more than confuse me. I have understood a few things at least from my research: it is *not* a closed-road bike course and it will involve fairly major roads and some tight corners. This means that going at full pelt while also remaining safe is at points unlikely to be possible, especially if the weather forecast is to be believed and we ride in the midst of thunderstorms.

At 5.20 a.m. exactly, Em and I meet by the lift and head down to the empty hotel lobby with our bikes. Together we cruise slowly along the side of the River Tyne.

'How's it feeling?' Em asks, eyes pointing at my rear tyre.

I had forgotten. Em replaced the dodgy back tyre for me last night in all of five minutes.

'Great,' I say. 'Thank you.'

We ride on for about two hundred metres before spotting a small group waiting by the collection point.

5.26 a.m. I get a stab of nerves. Thankfully the bus soon

arrives and about eight of us pile in as the driver grumpily fastens our bikes onto the trailer. It is now 5.40 a.m. and so far, though it is overcast, there has been no rain. Could it be that the weather gods are grinning again and I will get away with it just as I did in Blenheim?

We are heading north out of the city, rolling ever closer to the scene of my grand finale. A lady sitting next to Em is talking loudly about this Triathlon Championship and that Triathlon Series in a thick Glaswegian accent that reminds me a little of Jane Egan.

'So are you doing the tri today?' I ask.

'Ach no. I'm officiating,' she says. 'I work in the industry.'

'So you know all about it then?'

She nods.

'Any last-minute tips for someone just starting out?' I say.

'Yes,' she exclaims. 'Just *practise* your transitions.'

I'm not sure I would call that a useful last-minute tip.

'It's so funny!' the lady continues, becoming a little shrill. 'I see all these people in transition just getting everything wrong. They make such an arse of the whole thing. Like they put their T-shirt on inside out or they don't have the right shoes. The funniest thing I've seen is when people put their helmets on back to front! I mean, how stupid can you get?'

'It's all surprisingly easily done,' I mutter. 'When you're under pressure everything changes.'

'Ach yes, and that's why you should practise!' she says. 'You just go through it with your tri club. Time yourself. Over and over. There's no excuse really.'

I raise an eyebrow in Em's direction. She looks at me and

smiles. How can Em find this irritating woman funny? I try to repress my disproportionate fury at every person on this bus, reminding myself that I am wired and nervous and the combination makes me difficult and crazy.

We arrive at the venue and are dropped off right next to the Portaloos. An excellent opportunity, I think, and step into the nearest cubicle. I know from previous running events that such facilities are usually fairly unpleasant – long before the event begins the runners' nerves go to their intestines – so I'm holding my nose as I pull the door open. But nothing could have prepared me for the sight that greets me, as I barge in on a naked man sitting on the loo with a tri suit around his ankles.

Good start, I think, slamming the door closed with a squawk of apology.

I scuttle back to Em and tell her, amid very childish giggles, what happened.

'We have to get out of here,' I laugh. 'I've just seen my first naked man in about six and a half years and I feel all discombobulated.'

6.25 a.m. There is still an interminable eighty minutes until the first start wave will go. They begin at 7.45 and will do the sprint distance. Those of us choosing to attack today's longer distance, the 1500-metre swim, 46-kilometre ride and 9.1-kilometre run, will begin at 8.10. All too quickly I have signed a form and picked up a few sheets with my race number – 550 – on them. There are two stickers, one for the stem of the bike saddle and one for the front of my helmet, along with a flapping piece of paper that must be affixed to the race belt I'll put on in the first transition. Next I enter the transition zone to rack my bike and lay out all the things I'll need for the cycle ride and run whilst Em holds on to my wetsuit, swim cap and goggles.

Do I know where my bike is and how to find it quickly as I emerge from the two-hundred-metre run out of the water?

Check. Second row, about halfway up.

Are my cycle shoes in front of my running shoes, so that I can easily access them first? Absolutely; good.

Is my helmet just next to them – so that I remember to put it on *before* I touch my bike? Yes.

Is my race belt inside my helmet, so that I remember to put it on *after* my cycling top? No, but . . .

Wait – have I put the bike in the correct gear so that I can get away with the minimum of chain-clunking fuss? Yes. This is the first triathlon for which I've remembered this little trick.

6.58 a.m. I walk back to Em, pleased to have taken such care over this all-important set-up.

The clouds hang low over our heads and I recall the predicted storms, wishing that the whole damned thing would just bloody well start. A few stalls are opening to sell kit at knock-off prices but there is no sign of a coffee vendor and I could really use a pick-me-up.

Then it hits me.

'What's that *smell*?' I ask out loud, to nobody in particular.

A race official answers. 'It's the marsh water,' he says. 'Smells like sulphur, right?'

I nod. And I have to get into that water in about an hour's time.

Em is calm and quiet. She asks occasionally if I'm OK and whether I need anything from her but other than that we hang around in companionable silence as I bite my nails. There are three start waves beginning before mine, all of which are colour-coded by the assigned swim caps.

'Remember the plan,' I tell myself: 'Steady on the first lap of the swim and then pick up the pace on the second. Exactly the same goes for the bike. Steady on the first, pacey on the second.'

And then? I have no game plan for the run. Rob didn't say much about it, beyond ensuring I have enough energy in me to kick ass. It's more about survival and mental strength, I suppose; physically the run is more my strong suit than the cycling but it will almost certainly be the most painful part of this race since I failed to do even one of the six brick sessions Rob included in last month's training schedule. This run is also a three-lap course and laps are especially mentally challenging, for reasons that I'm about to discover.

I close my eyes and breathe. It will be over soon enough.

The smell is even stronger when I'm in the water.

'Sixty seconds!' someone behind a microphone yells.

Damn. My goggles are totally steamed up. The suncream that snuck into them in Lanzarote has rendered them fairly useless. I've been so busy taking my optician's advice and using my lensed goggles for swim sessions that I had forgotten how bad these ordinary goggles were.

'What an idiot,' I think. 'Why didn't I just buy a new pair when they first showed signs of failing?'

I pull them off my face and try to cup water into them to take the fog off whilst kicking my legs and tensing my abdominals to stay afloat. I repeat the same cycle about three times in thirty seconds. It is exhausting and does little to solve the issue.

I turn to a man who treads water next to me. 'Good luck,' I say.

'You too,' he nods. 'Have a good race.'

We are right up front. Though I know from experience now that there is often a respectful solemnity to these last seconds before a race begins, I am still surprised by the quiet that has descended upon the lake. I turn around and take a glance at the other competitors. Big mistake; I knew I shouldn't have done it but, a bit like looking down from a great height, couldn't resist. There are shoals and shoals of yellow-swim-capped heads hovering in a small amount of water. I'm sure there must be women here but right now I notice only male faces. How many? Two hundred maybe? In St Lucia we were eighty; in Hyde Park and Blenheim there were about fifty and sixty in each wave respectively. In Lanzarote there were more – around three hundred, including professionals – but there was also more space and the opportunity to hang back and begin from the beach rather than in the water.

'Twenty seconds!'

I turn my head back to face the race course, holding a large yellow buoy, the first turn point, in my sights. I berate myself again: why have I chosen to come forward and start up front? I'm going to get pummelled by these guys! It is far too late to begin edging back; I have no choice but to swim and see what happens.

The horn goes and that is exactly what I do. One, two, breathe. Always to the left side. I don't like the imbalance of gasping every two strokes but the adrenalin is pumping and my lungs are not yet ready for every three. Sure enough, people quickly pass me and I get sprayed, brushed and even shoved as we charge off. One man slips past on my right with a beautiful, efficient stroke style while another crashes about next to me for a few seconds before I leave him behind. As I splutter and splash my way through the first hundred metres I find myself imagining what we must look like from way, way above. A group of black and yellow water birds perhaps, or a patchy oil slick.

Unlike in previous races where I lifted my head out of the water to check my course occasionally, this time I'm adopting a submarine-esque viewing style. I tilt my eyes up onto the surface of the water like a periscope and can check my position with less disruption to my speed. As an added bonus, it also amuses me. You do what you have to, to get through the pressure and pain of race conditions, whether it's remembering a special person now passed, envisaging your favourite place or pretending to be a submarine detective who is about to take down the other swimmers and lock them up for good. But even my new trick leaves something to be desired today because I can only see clearly out of the very edge of each eyepiece so lose approximately eighty per cent of all vision whether my head is above or below water. I don't even arrive at the first turn point before I have to stop and look up to check position.

It is now during the last straight of the first lap that I get into my groove. I begin to focus on the all-important reach-and-rotate movement that helps my body to roll through the water and minimise drag and soon find myself breathing bilaterally and enjoying the weightlessness of wetsuited legs.

As I turn round the buoy that marks the end of the first 750 metres, I remember the plan to pick up the pace on the second lap and flutter my legs for a little boost of speed. I set an intention: go hard but not insane. There is plenty of time left for madness. Ren's voice rings disapprovingly in my head – *you're holding back, you pansy!* – but I ignore it, trusting myself, my experience and my body.

Swimmers bunch up at every turn point and each time I am forced to slow down and do breaststroke. Here it comes again, that unfriendly competitiveness as I find myself wanting to yell fiercely at those who dare to get in my way. I had intended to go wide around every buoy to avoid this infuriating congestion yet somehow it never happens.

'And I'm supposed to be drafting!' I think to myself about halfway round the second lap. 'Find someone fairly swift and try to tuck in behind and harness their speed.'

Drafting during swimming can save lots of energy – up to ten per cent if you draft from immediately behind and up to twenty per cent if you stay to the side and behind like a wingman – which in triathlon can be used on a later leg. It's a little cheeky but an entirely legal and sensible strategy, as that woman who stuck behind me demonstrated some six weeks ago at Blenheim Palace lake.

Turn points and drafting. Two carefully thought-out tactics that I have completely failed to remember until now.

I feel despondent for a moment, but then I hear . . .

Can we have a moment to appreciate how awesome you are right now?

I'm not sure whose voice it is. Rob's? Jane's even? It is certainly not Ren's: she might say something like 'If you've got the energy to self-congratulate then you're not going hard enough.'

But there it is again: *hey, remember . . . you can handle it.*

I feel suddenly that this voice isn't just one of my mentors but also a part of me. It's . . . *self-belief.* I've got to thirty-two years old and, although we've been introduced, I don't think self-belief and I have ever really got acquainted until this year. We've still got some work to do before we are the best of friends but there's no doubt that the effects of our meeting one another are limitless. They stretch out like open arms into other areas of my life: work, romance, friendships . . . Life is easier to handle with a greater sense of self.

So is triathlon, it appears: suddenly I'm in a better rhythm and I'm overtaking rather than being overtaken.

What seems like a few seconds later the ramp is beckoning to me. I keep swimming until my hands hit wood, not putting my feet down until I absolutely have to. Gliding in for those last few strokes is faster than wading. Today every second counts.

I pull myself out of the water. Running uphill in a wetsuit with water falling from every orifice is always disorientating. Yet this time I am conscious of it being less gruelling than at Blenheim or Hyde Park. On both of those occasions I felt debilitatingly dizzy but today I find myself far clearer than ever before. Still my speed is nowhere near that of the children I supported at the Hever Castle Triathlon two and a half weeks ago but for a fully grown woman wearing a thick, uncomfortable wetsuit it feels fairly punchy. Why? How? It's not as if I've practised this first transition – except of course in those previous race situations – but my confidence is tangible in comparison to then. I suppose I must be a fitter, better swimmer and so it takes a little less out of me. But then – was I pushing hard enough if I now feel relatively energetic? Could it be that I have found the balance between being fast enough to be out of the water in good time but not so effortful that I run up the hill like I have recently gulped down a bottle of wine? Finding these sweet spots is one of the biggest challenges of triathlon. Push, but not too soon. Hold back, but not too much.

This part took thirty minutes and forty-three seconds the last time I did it under race conditions, in Lanzarote. I certainly *felt* faster today but who knows? The proof will be in my official swim finish time but I won't get that until much later and there is plenty yet to do.

'Looking strong, Fry!' yells Em as I hotfoot it past and up, up, up into the transition area.

Later, I will find out that I swam twenty-eight minutes and forty-three seconds. That's two minutes faster than thirteen weeks ago at Volcano Tri, and means (were we to assume I swam the same time for both laps, which may or may not be correct) my 750-metre split time is actually *faster* than seven weeks ago in Hyde Park, where I only had to do 750 metres in total. It is also only nine minutes more than it took for me to swim half the distance eight months ago back in St Lucia. It remains a universe away from my old friend, ex-triathlete Olivia, who used to knock off the 1500-metre swim in under twenty-five minutes, or the professional female triathletes who usually do it in less than twenty. But still: happy days.

Now the cycle. After a relatively efficient outfit change – two minutes and sixteen seconds for the entire first transition – I jog my bike to the mount line, place one leg over the saddle and quickly find myself pedalling my way out of the Woodhorn Museum grounds and onto a main road. Rob has advised starting out in an easy gear, focusing on spinning my legs around at a high cadence, otherwise known to me as *bloody fast*.

I'm on the main road by the time I realise I have inadvertently put my race belt on before my cycling top because I forgot to lay it out in the correct place! It's actually a relief not to have the paper flapping in the wind and since nobody has stopped me for the offence – one *should* have the race number clearly showing on the back for the ride and the front for the run – I leave it there rather than stop and lose time adjusting it.

It takes me about ten minutes before I remember Rob's advice about how I should tuck down into a more energy-efficient position. By making myself smaller in this way not only am I less vulnerable to wind resistance but I also feel safer as the cars zoom past. I try to imagine my legs as mechanical pistons that just keep going no matter what. It can't be much after 9 a.m., still fairly early for a Saturday, but there are plenty of vehicles on the single carriageway already.

For the first half of the first lap, I find little to get excited about. I could be anywhere in the UK: the drivers' faces all look the same; in the distance the fields are flat and fairly unremarkable whilst above our heads the sky is the colour of limestone. For a minute here or there the rain begins and stops, begins and stops. The road surface isn't great either; there are no disasters like potholes but teeny-tiny bumps provide plenty of friction for my skinny tyres to work against. I struggle to maintain speed and power, just as I did in Blenheim, whilst others pass me by without a grimace.

Where am I going wrong? I ask myself. Have I missed something here? At least being overtaken by these people (mostly men) is a sure sign that I was quicker than them during the swim. But still.

'Forty-six kilometres of this?' I think. 'Poor Em. She could be waiting a long time.'

Despite all that I am feeling fairly upbeat. I might be tired of my own ineptness on a bike but I'm clearly not physically exhausted yet because I feel annoyed when I have to stop at roundabouts and traffic lights for ten, twenty seconds at a time. After about ten kilometres I follow the big cardboard arrows off a main road and onto a much smaller country lane and I am struck by one very positive thing: the cars and other cyclists hardly bother me these days. I feel secure on my bike. We are warned by marshals to slow down at one particularly narrow turning and, though I hit the brakes, I also lean to one side with my knee facing outwards so as to corner with a little speed.

The next section passes by in a blur of bends, small hills and pretty views. At one point we are directed through the village of Cresswell. The stark British beauty of this place gives me a huge boost. It is a Saturday morning in July and

I am cycling alongside the sea as it whips up in the wind, spitting tiny flecks of ocean across the sand into my face. Actually that's just rain. But the sentiment remains: I would never have come here, nor to the St Lucian waters or the windy Lanza hills, without the promise (or threat) of a triathlon.

I feel goose pimples bubbling on my skin and it's not just from the coastal gusts of cold air either. This is awe and appreciation. Can I harness the feelings to make me go faster?

Of course I can. And I will, on the run, I promise.

It is now that I think of Jane. This year she has won major races in Yokohama, Japan, Kitzbühel, Austria, and Franciacorta, Italy. She'll also be racing in three weeks' time at the British Paratriathlon World Championships in Liverpool. Less thrillingly, she is still waiting to hear if her disability category (PT1) is to be included in the line-up for the Paralympic in Rio in 2016. It is definitely included in the men's paratriathlon, but in the women's? That remains uncertain, and a decision won't be made until October at the earliest. Until then, Jane can only train, race and believe; train, race and hope.

If she can do all that, then I can damned well go up a gear right now. Not just that but I can simultaneously try to maintain the same cadence. Net result? I am now going slightly faster, albeit not totally all out yet. There's still a lot of the race to go.

Fifteen, maybe twenty minutes pass. There are wind turbines in view. This means I'm reapproaching the area near the Woodhorn Museum. Sure enough, a few surprisingly slow kilometres later I am riding past the entrance to the museum and a friendly marshal waves me on to begin my second lap. I push my legs a little harder, try to sustain a longer, stronger effort back to just before transition.

I am distracted momentarily as a woman who looks about my age and build cruises past. Her legs move slowly – she is in a high gear, I guess – and she remains ahead by about fifty metres for the next twenty minutes. I decide to use her as a pacer, agreeing with myself that I won't let her out of my sight until the end. Halfway round and just before that turn off the main road and onto the smaller one, she stops at a roundabout and I catch up, making use of a lucky break in traffic to zip past whilst she gets going.

'Ha! Take that!' I say under my breath to the high-gear woman.

It becomes a case of the tortoise and the hare. A short, steep hill arrives and the same woman slides past again without the merest hint of effort and remains ahead for the duration. I keep her within my sights but in the last few kilometres she loses me entirely.

I accept defeat, hoping to catch her on the run. Finally, the wind turbines come into view for the second time. Time to think about this next and final stage. Rob had some advice, something I was supposed to do around now. I scroll through my list of dos and don'ts until I remember:

When you think you are 2–3 km or maybe 5 minutes from the end you should start to ease off the pace. Also move around in your seat, stand up on the pedals and generally get the blood moving into other parts of your legs and body (not just your quadriceps) in preparation for the run. And have fun. Smile. It's contagious. I think it's a scientific fact that forcing yourself to smile and laugh, even if it is faked, elevates your mood measurably.

I smile and jiggle just like he told me. Easing off down the road that leads back into transition, I hear Em shout my name.

I catch her out of the side of my eye and smile. She is jumping up and down. No wonder – she's not the one who now has to run 9.1 kilometres. I had until this morning thought it would be 9.6 as advertised, but clearly a little remeasuring went on and the exact distance is five hundred metres less. Either way, a part of me feels disappointed. I'd have liked to run the full ten kilometres. Just to do the damned thing right.

The fastest athletes will be finishing around now, I think with envy. I rack my bike and take a last gulp of water before changing my shoes. A quick suck of a gel as I move one foot first and then the other and it begins. I'm almost on course to meet Rob's recommendations – perhaps a hundred or so calories shy, but on the whole I've been refuelling enthusiastically.

Time to dig deep, as my triathlon friends might say. Or to go hard or go home. To never, ever give up. It's going to hurt. It already does. There is a brief downhill before I am marshalled to the left along a dirt track that hugs the lake I was swimming in about two hours ago. My legs feel as if I am wearing ankle weights. I distract myself with a few calculations – I know that with a determined mind and dogged legs I am able to come off the bike and run ten kilometres in fifty minutes. How much can I shave off that, given it is nine hundred metres less today?

With all the blood rushing to my muscles it is hard to do any kind of simple maths. It takes me until the far corner of the lake to break the numbers down. Maybe I can do it in forty-five minutes? It is ambitious but feasible, especially since I have overtaken at least three women already, one of whom wears a green tri suit that I'm sure I noticed overtaking me at the very beginning of the cycle ride. There is a nod of acknowledgement as I pass and I can't help but enjoy a little schadenfreude. Green-trisuit lady has thick, powerful thighs that cast shadows over mine. Her heavy muscles stole time and miles from me on the cycle ride but now add kilograms that make her slower on the run. It is the fairest and most frustrating thing about triathlon. Your strengths can be your weaknesses; you get ahead, you fall behind. As if to demonstrate this further, a man flies past green-trisuit lady and me at unimaginable speed. He is whippet thin, almost gaunt, with feet that dance across the ground as if it were moving underneath him. It's unusual to see this kind of disparity in ability at this stage in a race but it does happen; he is probably a committed runner who has turned up today to give our multi-disciplined sport a go. Now he gets to shine whilst the rest of us jog on. He will be done in forty minutes, I guess.

Directly opposite the lake from the transition and finish area is a small car park. Can I really only be halfway round the first lap? How long have I been running for? I should have worn a stopwatch but I don't have a waterproof one and putting one on in transition seemed like an extraordinary waste of seconds.

After a half mile or so along a narrow path encased by

shrubbery, I cross a tiny railway track. For a hundred metres I am alone, with only my laboured breathing and the rustle of my feet landing on mud for company. There is a metal frame in the distance and through it I can see people. As I get closer I realise that one of those people is Em.

'Amaaaazing!' she yells. 'You look fantastic!'

These are almost certainly lies. What a truly wonderful friend is Courier Em. I push a fist up into the air and run past, aware that I am far from the finish line. This is why running laps of any course requires such mental endurance. Though it can facilitate a faster time as one learns the lie of the land via the first lap and then knows, particularly on the last, how much remains and when to push, it is for similar reasons excruciating. The first time I pass a landmark or a marshal on the track around the lake, my main thought is 'I have to pass you two more times before this pain is over.' As is usually the way with lap courses we are now forced to run towards two arrows, one marked 'Final lap – to finish line' and the other marked 'Second and third laps'. Ouch. Would it be such a terrible thing if I just slipped over to the right? I could say it was a mistake, that I had in my exhaustion simply 'forgotten' how many laps I had done?

It is not a real consideration, more a kind of playful imagining designed to help me remember why I'm here. What it does instead, however, is momentarily divert my focus, just enough that I wonder if I have in fact gone the right way. I am now running uphill inside the grounds of the Woodhorn Museum and I can hear the cheer of crowds as finishers cross the line. In a sudden fit of total disorientation, I stop. A gel falls from my pocket onto the ground. I reach behind to pick it up. That's at least ten seconds gone. I left my brain back by the railway line. I have no idea where I am.

'Hey!' I yell out to an oncoming runner. 'What lap are you on? Is this the right way for lap two?'

He looks as disorientated as me. 'I'm finishing,' he says and races past.

I ask the woman behind him the same question. She is more helpful: 'I'm going onto lap two.'

Confused and frustrated, I continue in the same direction. Standing for at least thirty seconds has caused my legs to seize a little. I stop by the water table for a few moments, taking a full glass and walking as I drink. Though I want to chug the lot I am cautious not to take too much; it could bloat my stomach, give me a stitch or, worst of all, a bad tummy (there's a reason why they call it 'having the runs' after all) . . .

It takes some time to settle back into running and I am quarter of the way through my second lap before, composure regained, I start assessing how I'm doing. How am I feeling, I ask myself, and what can those feelings tell me about my temporal whereabouts, not to mention the possibility of speeding up during the last lap? Over the years of running I have gathered a strange understanding of the variation between 'felt time' and 'real time'. Felt time becomes an entity and a measure in itself, which in turn helps 'real time' to be gauged. It's a bit like an X and a Y axis. On the few occasions that I have done long, slow runs, for example – say between ninety minutes and two hours – the relationship of those two axes has changed as the run goes on. At the beginning felt and real time are approximately equal. Then it shifts, around fifteen or twenty minutes after starting, as my body struggles to find itself. The X (felt time) axis is a little inversely proportional to Y (real time). That's usually when running feels unpleasant. But then the heart rate settles a little and the natural endorphins begin to flow, something magical occurs and the relationship between the axes is reversed: it feels like twenty minutes and yet forty-five have actually floated past. It is how I imagine trail runners must feel sometimes, when they breathe and bounce themselves up a mountain. But though I have during rare hours experienced that blissful time-versus-perceived-time disparity, it has never occurred during a run in a triathlon. Generally speaking, races are races and there is no time for steady rhythms and peaceful flow, especially not for rookies like me. Sure enough, today I am in the predictable space where felt time is higher than real time. So if it feels like half an hour since I racked my bike it probably isn't. Actually, the fact that it feels like half an hour right now probably means that it is not much more than twenty minutes. Maybe twenty-two. Yes, that's more like it. Twenty-two or twenty-three.

My body can go faster than this, at least one minute per mile faster. I am as certain of this as I am of my name and the fact that triathletes are a madcap bunch. But that doesn't mean that I can actually go faster at this point in time, because my mind is not on board. I feel exhausted and just a tiny bit like giving up, so I decide to simply focus on holding this pace, not slowing down.

My spirits are lifted about one third of the way round the second lap by the sight of a walking man bent double over his torso. Offering him one of three remaining gels from my back pocket – yelling, 'It's a spare!' – as I run past gives me the boost I need to keep my pace up until the midway point. Now it's my turn. Here, as planned, I pull out my favourite gel from my back pocket. Oh sweet nectar! Its ingredients are standard – primarily sugar and caffeine – but this brand of toffee-coffee flavouring is surprisingly hard to find in high-street sports shops and tastes far better than the rest. I only had one left at home and brought it up to Newcastle, saving it for this precise moment. By the time I am approaching the end of the second lap I can feel the effects. My legs are more achey than ever and yet seem to have more energy in them than at the start. From the outside it probably looks more like a crawl but the shift up a gear feels to me like I've taken off.

I see Emily for a second time. She is standing in exactly the same place and says exactly the same thing. Next time I see her, I think, I'll be on the last hundred metres. So nearly there. One more agonising lap to go.

I start to set my sights on runners up ahead and pick them off. One by one by one I pass them as they trudge onwards towards the finish. I know it's hardly representative of how good I am – the speedier triathletes are way ahead or chugging glucose drinks in the finish area – but it bolsters the self-esteem and fuels me more than any carbohydrate could. But wait – another skinny man who has stopped by the side of the course to rest!

'Nearly there, buddy,' I say.

He shakes his head, a vague blueish hue, the mark of dehydration, around his lips.

'You can't give up now. It's your last lap?'

He nods.

I reach into my back pocket. One more left – my emergency last-resort gel – just in case something terrible happens to my energy levels in this last three kilometres. I stop for about five seconds.

'Go on, take it,' I urge.

He does, beginning to open it with his teeth, and before even one drop has reached his mouth he starts to run. I knew there was a reason I brought six of those instead of four! But now, back to my race. I have to focus wholeheartedly on me, my legs, my lungs, in these final horrible minutes. The felt-time-versus-real-time disproportion gets even bigger for the last half mile or so. It feels like an hour and three quarters since I started running, probably more than double the real time. What does it feel like, I wonder, to actually run for an hour and three quarters in a triathlon? That's what Ren has done, in a Half Ironman. And double that – much more than double – is what's required in an Ironman, straight after a 180-kilometre cycle ride. In one week's time Suzanne will be doing exactly that in Zurich, Switzerland. She will be running more than four times what I'm doing here and, right now, I can't imagine how that is possible. Certainly not for me. I cannot see these legs surviving. I'm probably around eight kilometres in and I can already hear myself breathing like a seal.

Is this the hurt locker? I wonder. It feels like it, but I suspect my mind is not yet strong enough to go there. I think I could be on track for forty-five minutes in the run but I've forgotten all the short stops to check directions, my two walks through the water stations and the small inclines and many corners of the beginning and end of laps.

How much difference can it make?

Here I am again. The final straight in the shadowy lane with overgrown bushes on each side. Cross the railway tracks. Continue on past walkers – bastards who have finished their race already – coming the other way. There are no thoughts of other triathletes any more, no motivating phrases inside my mind. All I can hear, see, think or feel is get-to-the-end-and-make-it-stop. Feet moving forward. Seal-breath in and out. Where is Em? She is not in her usual place. I am approaching it. Have passed it. No sign of Em. Up the horrible short hill that leads me back to the museum hub and then – yes! – there she is, camera poised, screaming at the top of her lungs:

'GO FRY GO FRY GO FRY!'

When you have a short surname people use it. I have never been so grateful for that as I am now. It's much more motivational than just 'Go Lucy'. Seeing Em adds an engine to my rear end. I no longer have bird wings but those of an aeroplane.

'GO FRY!'

She is behind me now. Ahead I see only one woman, heading towards the finish. I am gaining on her.

What's the point? says knackered brain.

Because you can, says another part.

One more person. I can do it. I sprint headlong towards her. Overtake her. Sprint down one more straight to cheers of 'G'wan Shordie' from all around. For a moment I wonder who they are talking to. Shordie? Is it Geordie for Shorty? Could it be me they're cheering? But I'm not short. I'm –

Finished. 2.55 says the clock.

'G'wan Shordie! Nice one Shordie!'

Perhaps it is a term of endearment. Right now it doesn't matter. Call me whatever you like. I've just finished my final – and fastest – triathlon. I am invincible, I am sky-high.

'You're a hero!' says Em when we are reunited.

'Very sweet,' I smile: she has been primed. 'I need water.'

'Seriously.' She grins. 'This is amazing. I want to do it!'

'Excellent.' Another sporty female inspired by triathlon. 'Let me find water.'

Almost immediately, the intense discomfort is gone. It is with incredible simplicity that it happens. Continue to run = continue to feel pain. Stop running = stop feeling that same pain. Within a minute or so my breathing calms down and I start chatting to race organisers and other finishers.

There isn't much I wouldn't volunteer for right now. I don't know if I am particularly susceptible to the tongue-loosening properties of endorphins but one old gym buddy of mine used to say that there was a dangerous ten-to-fifteen-minute window after we had finished working out when I would turn acquaintances into friends, enemies back into acquaintances, and plot grandiose plans with anyone who would listen.

Suffice to say that I am used to getting high on exercise. But today the joy of the aftermath is accompanied by an extra-potent flush of happy juice. Is this the end of an incredible journey or is there more to come?

'Maybe I should do a Half Ironman,' I say out loud, just to myself.

But, thankfully, I know I should wait a few days before making any decisions. Never commit to any future race in the immediate aftermath of one.

Around twenty minutes later, when I am rehydrating and have my mouth around a huge cheese and ham crêpe, I have almost entirely forgotten the distress of the run. I am doped on endorphins. Wrapped in wellbeing. There is nothing so good as this moment, this feeling: it is excitement without the jumpiness, calm without the quiet and accomplishment without hubris.

Em and I watch the winners take their places and accept their prizes on the makeshift podium. The female winner of the standard distance that took me two hours and fifty-five minutes completed it in two hours, eighteen minutes and thirty seconds. Pretty impressive stuff! Here is how this first lady, Hazel Smith of Edinburgh Tri Club, did it: she spent nearly eight minutes less in the water than I did and was over a minute faster than me on the first transition. She put nineteen minutes between us on the bike and then gained on me by another twenty-nine seconds in the bike-to-run transition. To top it all off, Smith did the 9.1-kilometre run eight minutes and eighteen seconds faster than my forty-seven minutes and forty-eight seconds.

🏃

I try to calculate my improvements. Measuring achievement on finishing times alone is difficult in triathlon. In St Lucia, the organisers insisted the cycle course was so hilly that 13.5 kilometres here was equivalent to twenty somewhere else. Today, we had six kilometres more to cycle than in a true Olympic-distance triathlon and nearly a kilometre less to run. In Blenheim the run was not just 5.7 kilometres, as opposed to the usual five in a sprint distance, it was also undulating. River swims can include a current but lake swims are usually fairly comparable. Even then, the placement of the buoys and number of turns can alter one's speed enough to make a difference to those athletes who are focused on shaving off seconds.

For those of us who are far from winning it isn't always easy to be certain of good performance. Even age-group rankings are dubious since the strength of the field of competitors is largely arbitrary too. But still, there are generalisations that can be made. Under three hours for an Olympic distance is good in an average kind of way. It means you are fit, clearly committed to training and can perform consistently over three disciplines. Two and a half hours and you're really competing, most likely in the top twenty of your age group, perhaps even top ten. If you finish between two hours and two hours fifteen then you're elite, perhaps a professional athlete. These are simplifications, often inaccurate, but they are as close as I have got to some kind of correlation between speed, time and ability in the complex sport of triathlon.

Two hours and eighteen minutes, I marvel, reflecting again on today's winning time in the female race. How long has she been racing? I wonder. How much quicker could I get with a few years' solid training behind me?

Not that quick, I strongly suspect. But there's more here, if I want it. And do I? Right now what I want most in the world is for this crêpe that is bubbling with hot cheese to *not* be nearly finished. I try to push the thought of triathlon away but it hovers around my mind like one of those lazy summer flies: *More here if you want it.*

16

I wake up the next day with a small amount of stiffness and a message from Suzanne:

I was reflecting a bit after our chat, as I tend to do. Although my training schedule seems big, compared to the men I watched toiling under the Indian sun when I was travelling there . . . in 40 degrees centigrade, making bricks by hand all day for their whole working lives . . . gym and swim in air-conditioned comfort with filtered water on tap seems like the right end of the stick. Even if I exercise five hours a day, I'm still on my butt or asleep for almost three times as many hours that day. (Speaking of exercise – we did 4.2 km in the pool today and it's breakfast time.)

I roll over and smile. No more swimming for me today. I've done my job and it feels amazing. Maybe it's just relief or perhaps it is a nutritional thing – I certainly refuelled enthusiastically after the race, and took on high-quality protein every three to four hours until bedtime on Saturday night – or perhaps it's good karma for being a gel-fairy, but I am surprised at how bouncy I feel, almost like I could do the entire swim–bike–run race again today.

That morning I stroll around Newcastle in a very good mood. After lunch I head out of the city to the beautiful coastal town of Tynemouth to meet a friend for a relaxed

Sunday afternoon walk along the beach.

'I hardly hurt!' I tell her with disbelief.

There has been a fallout with each of my previous triathlons. Sometimes it takes hours. Other times it sinks in overnight. But it is always here by now. This time it's weird. I actually feel better than I did after both recent sprint events, despite having been on the go for nearly double the amount of time.

Have I got away with it?

No. On Monday afternoon when I return home an insidious kind of lethargy arrives, made up partly of muscle soreness and partly of neurological fatigue. It starts in the morning with an empty, drained feeling in the limbs. On the train I sit and stare out of the window, uncharacteristically unable to read or write. I know what this is: the central nervous system takes a battering during triathlon and is effectively traumatised for a while after. By the time I put my key in the lock I am achey, uncreative and irritable. Something hurts. Something twitches and the glands in my throat are a bit inflamed. I am exhausted but struggle to sleep deeply. I am pleased to be home, reunited with Bella and our podgy ginger tomcat, but the enthusiasm I usually feel for life, triathlon – even for my wife and cat – is dulled.

~~◠~~

One long sleep back in my own bed and I feel brighter. By Wednesday, I am fully revived. I spend the next few weeks enjoying a return to the gym for some resistance training and even make it to the pool once for a long swim. I do not get back on my bike and I do not go for a run. But as much as I try and ignore it, the tricky question of triathlon hangs around. What will I do now? More pressingly, what are my triathlete friends doing? The season is far from over – there is still August and early September left before its official end, and just because my body and money are both spent for one year doesn't mean everyone else's are too.

A week after my efforts in Newcastle Suzanne hits a high of her own at Ironman Zurich, taking a full forty-five minutes off her personal best for an Ironman with an overall race time of twelve hours, thirty-two minutes and twenty-three seconds. I ask her for the details. She tells me she didn't enjoy much of the race, as she usually does, partly because of the rainy cold weather and partly due to seeing a nasty high-speed bike crash (the rider left unconscious, bleeding from the head). Her pacing went to plan though and she'll be resting her now-swollen ankles for a few days rather than having every spare hour accounted for.

Whilst Suzanne rests, Jodie's training intensifies. With around five weeks to go until tapering starts two weeks before Ironman Wales (taking place mid September), there's still plenty to be achieved. Some thorny personal issues come along and knock her sideways. But Ironman allows for little distraction. Jodie has to make a decision to refocus and recommit, and fast, if she's to be ready in time.

'I might not win,' she tells me after a few days of missed training sessions, 'but I'm still going to do it. I've put too much in to give up now. My grandma used to say to me: you work hard, you become someone. That always sticks in my mind.'

I keep my fingers crossed for both Jodie and her main competitor, Hollie. They both deserve the prize but only one of them can win. And as Jodie and Hollie battle it out for a place at Kona, Paula will be racing around her first Olympic-distance triathlon in the Scottish Borders. She's recently cranked up her training to four or five sessions per week, she tells me when we meet in Edinburgh in early August. She knows she can't just wing it fitness-wise, as she has done for the sprint distance events.

'But guess what?' she says, switching tone from downcast to upbeat. 'Remember how much I hated swimming in St Lucia?'

'Yes,' I say. 'I'm fairly sure we bonded over that!'

'I can't believe it. I totally love it now. I had a few lessons and something switched.'

This time it's running she finds the toughest, Paula says, but she's determined to do it. She has to get the miles under her feet.

'You know, exactly the same thing happened to me,' I say.

We continue to share our swim transformations. We are both amazed how it is that, with a little instruction and perseverance, we have gone from sinking-potato-sack swimmers who fight aggressively against the water to roll-ing-boats-with-paddles who try to keep slender and glide through. Of course there's a long way to go before we start hitting really decent swim times for 1500 metres, like those clocked by Suzanne and Emily, but who cares? I hope that maybe Bella will get the swimming bug too; I'd love for us, come next spring, to head out of London together early on Sunday mornings for swims in lakes and rivers.

As for Ren? After a supposedly great amount of pleading from friends (read: a couple of pints and the suggestion that she's gone soft), Ren has agreed to take part in the Great Kindrochit Challenge. A quadrathlon held in the Scottish highlands next July, it's a one-day endurance test consisting of a 1.35-kilometre swim, twenty-five-kilometre run (or hike, over seven Munroes), eleven-kilometre kayak and fifty-four-kilometre cycle. But for now, it's business as usual at CrossFit, with plenty of (running) track sessions thrown in.

A couple of weeks later, I also connect with Jane. Despite still nursing that elbow niggle, she's been powering through the World Championship Paratriathlon Series. She scored a second-place finish in the European Championships in Kitzbühel in June and most recently has won the British Paratriathlon Championships in Liverpool, a few days ago.

'What's next on the agenda, Champ?' I ask, using my favourite nickname for my new friend.

'Well, there's Edmonton, at the end of this month. That's the last of the World Series. Then in October I'll find out if my category – PT1 – is going to be included in the Paratriathlon at the 2016 Olympics. If it is, then the qualifying period begins in 2015.'

'Amazing,' I say, a little scared of what happens in October if Jane's category isn't included. 'Lots of wins but . . . how have things actually been, otherwise, you know?'

She inhales.

'Actually I've had a couple of really bad weeks,' she says. 'I had a great week after returning from Italy and then the next week I had a massive pain flare-up and was a wreck . . .'

What followed was a fast and frightening spiral downwards, Jane explains. It went on for two weeks, a while after the pain subsided. It was, she says, the worst depression she had experienced in a long time – without a doubt. Then, all of a sudden, it just went away.

'Just like that?'

'Yeah,' she says. 'You know, I was on the verge of saying it's too hard, I'm not doing this any more.'

'It? You mean . . .'

'I didn't feel like paratri was helping me,' Jane says. 'It suddenly felt like it was too difficult for me, something I don't need in my life. Because I still felt like I had to train, people were sending me stuff to do, wanting the best for me – I felt like I was letting people and myself down.'

It's a double-edged sword, Jane agrees. 'My coach kept making arrangements to meet up with me to force me to still get out of bed and be normal and helped me through, so in some ways paratri actually got me out of it, but when I'm in that terrible place I feel like it's something I don't want. And there's always the fear that it won't go away this time . . . whenever the black stuff arrives. Tinged with that is the annoyance that you thought it might not come back and now it has. I find it a really frightening thing. Not only is it depressing in itself but it's doubly depressing because I know what it feels like to be well.'

'Yes, of course,' I say, understanding, in my own way, the agonising nostalgia for simple joy that one often feels when a cloud so dark arrives as to completely block the view.

A few days later I head out for a run. It's the first time I've tied up the laces on these shoes since transition at the Newcastle event. That was almost a month ago now and there has been a definite trajectory in my feelings about the sport during the course of those four weeks. First, rest and relief. An overwhelming sense of freedom at *not* having to try and follow a training programme, *not* having to worry about an upcoming event. Second, a desire to go back to some higher-intensity, sweaty training and a sadness at having to return the turbo trainer to Emily. Third, a strong impulse to spend time with both Ren and Rob, whom I miss in very different but equal ways. Fourth, that annoying buzzing. Should I? Shouldn't I? Is it over for me and tri? Something still tells me: there is more here if I want it.

In a way that would previously have been unthinkable to me, I decide to let the answers come in their own time, rather than wrestling with them to make them appear right now. I'll enjoy the off season and then decide. Like Rob says, if I miss triathlon so much, I'll go back to it. If not, then I've done something (five things, actually) that I wasn't ever sure I'd do.

I'm halfway around the local common when I start to notice a little tiredness in my legs. I don't really care – the first three kilometres felt fantastic and it's to be expected after some time off. It's a bright, sunny day after a dramatic storm and for a moment I thought I smelt the slight oakiness of early autumn.

As I move off the path and onto a more forgiving, muddy track, I think of Jane, remembering our recent conversation. I wonder how she's doing – what she's doing – right now, at this very moment. I hope 'the black stuff' hasn't returned yet but suspect, sadly, that she has too much to tackle for it not to arrive, unwanted, at some point again in the future.

Is triathlon worth it? I ask myself as I try and ignore the impulse to stop running and take a breather. *A hundred times over*, is the unhesitant answer that comes back, not just from Jane's imaginary voice inside my head but also from my own. During the last twelve months I've played with, and battled against, triathlon to emerge a slightly different – I'd say more contented – person. I don't think it's visible from the outside – my physique hasn't drastically altered – but in other ways I have completely outgrown my own costume. Facing fears, big and small, has given birth to a self-belief that spills over like gold into other areas of my life. I say yes to things more readily. But I am also better at tempering my expectations of myself and differentiating between performance (or constant improvement) and intrinsic worth. My pressure cooker has been switched on and off but no huge damage has been done – perhaps I've even learned to work the damned thing better. What's more, the Relationship Crisis Barometer readings are at an all-time low, as Bella and I have come through the experience more united and with a greater affection and gratitude for the differences between us than ever before.

'What would I tell myself?' I think as I wipe my forearm against my brow. 'If I could go back in time one year, what might I say to me?'

The message comes quickly, clearly and from the heart as well as my sweaty head:

If in doubt, rest. Otherwise, trust the training. Always make friends with fear.

[257]

For every triathlete, it must be different. The inspirational people and phrases we choose to draw upon, the memories we make are never exactly the same. Yet, as I jog onto another muddy path, I begin to wonder if there is something – somewhere – within triathlon that we share. Where, exactly, do we find the essence of this sport? The answer, I think, is somewhere in transition. Not only is triathlon itself still in a state of ongoing transformation, growing in popularity and scope with such speed that it is impossible to capture and pin down, but it's also in this no-man's-land between disciplines that we see it most clearly. Not just in the arms of those who rip wetsuits off while on the run and in the legs of those who sprint hard straight off the saddle, but also in the way it takes its protégés from one place to another in their lives: from lacking in confidence to full of conviction; from apologetically hopeful to furiously – and sometimes indiscriminatingly – ambitious.

As I trudge on down the path, I ask myself, for at least the hundredth time: what is it about triathlon that makes so many of us fall in love with it? I've merely touched the edges of its appeal, yet there's one thing I'm certain of and that's the presence of contrast and contradiction. On a purely physical level, for example, the painful and potentially problematic curve of the upper back caused by hours of cycling is counteracted by plenty of swimming (a decent front-crawl technique helping the joints in that area to mobilise). Much in the same way that those blessed with a body naturally predisposed to swimming can't simultaneously be blessed with a body naturally predisposed to running, so too triathlon is the ultimate sporting juxtaposition. It is quintessentially contemporary by way of logistics and gadgetry, and yet noticeably timeless in the sheer physical rigour that it demands. It is about freedom for some and entrapment for others; health and fitness for some, addiction and illness for others. Triathlon requires every bit as much as it gives and yet somehow, paradoxically, it gives more than it requires. It is as great as it is greedy. As welcoming as it is cliquey. As tough as it is telling. It is a hotbed of competition and I hate it. It is liquid sunshine and I love it.

There is always more there if you want it.

Epilogue

It is late September, ten weeks since Newcastle Triathlon, and Bella and I are in the middle of a much-needed holiday in Greece. I'm sitting on some astroturf at the end of a wooden jetty, leaning awkwardly to one side with a waterski dangling over the edge. It's early – around 8 a.m. – and the water is calm, making small lip-smacking sounds as it hits the edge of the pontoon.

Finally I'm starting to relax. Thoughts of work, traffic, finances and the endeavours of the past year are becoming smaller with each sun-dappled day that passes, each plate of meze that's consumed.

I'm just about to drop into the sea and take hold of the tow-rope handle when Roley, my instructor, yells out:

'So, are you here for the triathlon next week?'

'What?' I yell back.

Surely I've misheard. This is a holiday resort, not a . . .

'There's a tri-training camp coming out next week. So we're putting on a triathlon and regular resort guests can join,' he says. 'You should do it. It's just in the harbour in town. You can do a super-sprint or a sprint. It's a really relaxed race. Free! And lots of fun.'

Triathlon is many things. Many wonderful things. But after a couple of months to reflect on my experiences of the sport I'm now more sure than ever that 'fun' isn't the first word that comes to mind. Nor is 'free', come to think of it.

We head out into the bay. The sunlight begins to dry the droplets on my arms as I tense and grip, carving in and out of the speedboat's wake.

It should be enjoyable. Would be, in fact, except I'm barely aware of skimming the frothy water, so loud are the thoughts in my mind about *triathlon* and *free*. About *next week* and *fun*.

'I probably should do it,' I think, leaning my weight onto the left edge of the ski.

'Why?' I think next, now shifting my weight right and zipping across to the other side. 'This is a holiday, remember?'

I haven't come to Greece for *shoulds*. I've come to play tennis and go paddleboarding, and to lie on a sun lounger reading the novels that have been piling up on my bedside table for the last few months. Maybe I've even come to swim a little in open water. But I haven't come to push my body through pain, nor to fight with my mind against my muscles' desire to stop. Triathlon is not on my agenda. And just because there happens to be a random event taking place here next week, it doesn't mean I have to do it.

Ten days later and it's the beginning of October. Terrible storms are forecast for tomorrow but today is beautiful – not a cloud in view – and the temperature a manageable twenty-five degrees. I stand near the start line of the twenty-third International Sivota Triathlon and enjoy the sun's warmth upon my skin. After the initial irritation of being chased around the Aegean by triathlon, I had become rather excited about doing just one more race before the year was out. But earlier this morning I made the decision *not* to race. It's partly the residual tiredness I feel after completing a 2.2-kilometre organised swim through some very choppy waters yesterday morning, but mostly it's my hip. During a hilly run last week I managed to aggravate the previous injury. The discomfort has been building for a few days and I can now feel it with every step I take. Of course, I tried to ignore it but whilst listening to the eccentric race briefing yesterday afternoon – *at the bike turnaround you may meet Monty-the-horse, who we call the Draft Master* – it became wholly apparent that to run would mean the risk of damaging myself.

I am disappointed but know it's the right decision. And perhaps choosing to rest rather than charge through injury is a victory itself. Maybe I am finally learning to take the longer-term view advocated by Rob, to treat small injuries as if they were big ones, as Suzanne once advised. Maybe I've proved what I needed to prove.

Besides, today is Bella's turn. For the months leading up to this holiday I watched her become increasingly worn out by work and run down by urban life, but in the twelve days that we have been away her stressed-out soul has softened, just as her face has freckled and her lethargy lifted. Without the pressure of hourly meetings and endless emails, she has recaptured a lost energy. She's had a swimming lesson and been for a few short runs. She's even been on two organised cycle rides, one of which she enjoyed and the other she totally hated. Now, without any prompting from me, she's decided to enter the super-sprint event and it seems fitting that this time our roles should be reversed. Me: cheerleader. Bella: triathlete.

It takes place by the town's harbour, little more than a five-minute cycle ride from our resort, so the logistics are easy too. It is exactly as promised – even more of a low-key, fun-focused affair than Tri St Lucia and with around only thirty participants getting ready. So relaxed is it that I'm allowed in transition to help Bella set up her things. It's a far cry from the transition area in the Hyde Park or Blenheim Triathlons, where temporary wire fences separated competitors from supporters and I had to flash my race number to be granted entry. Today, transition is little more than a small green space near the town's main roundabout by the water's edge. Plastic chairs from a local taverna provide a surface against which competitors can prop their bikes. Those who have been here all week as part of the organised triathlon training camp are using road bikes brought from home but hotel guests have been lent mountain bikes belonging to the resort. Just as well, since Bella is a cautious (read: fearful and inexperienced) cyclist who needs every extra piece of stability that a thick tyre can bring.

There really isn't much to do in transition; the water is warm and Bella won't be swimming in a wetsuit, nor does she have any cycling shoes. It's just a case of reminding her to don her helmet before touching her bike (that being the one firm rule that does still apply here) and to have a full water bottle on it.

I wave Bella off five minutes before the start. She's wearing bikini bottoms and a sports bra and clutching a swim cap and goggles. Despite having noticeably improved her front crawl during the course of the holiday, she's determined to do breaststroke throughout the three-hundred-metre super-sprint swim.

'I just want to relax and enjoy it,' she says.

I nod – I know this is code for *front crawl still frightens me a bit* – and give her shoulder a big squeeze before saying goodbye.

As the swimmers gather in the water, I head over to the taverna to get a coffee. It's the strongest money can buy; I need something to placate the triathlete in me, suddenly furious that I am injured and cannot compete. As I gulp it down I think of Paula, who had to pull out of her Scottish Borders triathlon due to injury. I wish she were here now and able to compete – I think she'd like the understated set-up, the laughter and sunshine. My thoughts also return to Jane. A few days ago she relayed the devastating news that her disability category has not been selected for inclusion in the 2016 Paralympics. This means she won't have the opportunity to try to qualify and represent her country, and perhaps, given her funding will be cut, she'll never race again. I know that this is a disappointment of epic proportions which will have life-altering effects. I am reminded of life's lottery and how my having the option to pull out of today's race, last minute, is actually more a privilege than a problem.

～●～

'Three, two, one, GO!'

It's time. Off they go, forming that scene of bobbing swim

caps that I have come to know and love, and it's not long until I'm clapping loudly as Bella comes out of the water, a grin stretching across her face. She heads over to her bicycle with a leisurely gait that reminds me of my performance in St Lucia. It is inconceivable now that I might approach transition in this slow and chirpy way, so lacking in urgency. Will Bella ever progress so far into the frenzied world of triathlon that she might become similarly consumed by the need for speed at every juncture? Unlikely, I suspect, but you never know. Today, certainly, she's remaining calm. She takes it very easy on the bike, disappearing slowly around the roundabout and out of town. I go back to the taverna to buy another coffee and watch the other competitors come by. Bella's cycle ride is just ten kilometres but I know she'll take it steady and probably won't be back for at least twenty-five minutes.

Though this event is far more intimate and informal than most, there are aspects to it that I'm sure are universal to every triathlon. These include, most crucially, a sense of endeavour, of people going beyond their physical and mental comfort zones. People who will never be quite the same again. Me, Ren, Suzanne and Emily. Jodie and Paula and Jane. And now it applies to my wife too. I know she will be changed ever so slightly by doing something so arguably pointless and excessive. So primal, yet so pedantic.

Here she comes, riding slowly through a small street with shops and cafes on either side.

'Yeah! Looking good, babe! Bravo!'

I scream encouraging words loudly and joyfully, the way Courier Em did in Newcastle and Bella did at the Hyde Park and Blenheim events.

I feel relieved. I know immediately from the smile on her face that there were no huge dramas on the bike. The biggest worry over, there's now just the straightforward matter of a three-kilometre run.

She starts out strong, with determination and a heavy smack of each foot as it hits the ground.

'What is she thinking?' I wonder. 'How does she feel?'

It is two laps; she passes me once and the second time I see her it's nearly over. She is red-faced and sweaty and her arms drop a little lower by her sides as she tries, obviously weary, to add a final increase in speed to those last fifty metres. I whoop and holler as she crosses the finish line.

It is a sight I never thought I'd witness.

One by one the other finishers run past. There's a female 'age-grouper' triathlete who has been taking part in the tri-training camp this week. I watch as she zooms to victory as the first female finisher, impressed not just by her speed but also that she has maintained it despite taking a nasty tumble turning a corner on the last lap, so her leg is now covered in blood. Her friend explains that she is blind in one eye; this kind of fall often happens when she's competing. Clearly it does little to disrupt her focus. Only one man has beaten her in today's race, but I sense it's one too many.

The next few speedy sprinters come in, with hands aloft. There is an ominous quiet before the less experienced tri-athletes arrive. A smiley woman in her late forties struggles through. Close behind is a fifty-something marathon run-ner, a social worker, accompanied, for the last fifty metres anyway, by her husband and nineteen-year-old son, who have both already finished. There are countless others too, who stumble or storm towards the end. Some are super fit and others less so. Some larger, some smaller, some relatively experienced at driving themselves through the pain of a triathlon and others, like Bella, for whom just getting round is a completely new experience. One thing unites them all: the same exuberant, slightly crazed grin that I wore at the end of each swim–bike–run event that I completed. Our faces send a message: weary bones and mangled muscles don't last, but our triathlon story will.

Acknowlegements

My darling Bella, I'll start with you, partly because I'm afraid of what might happen if I don't but also because without your unfailing belief in me, I'm not sure I'd have arrived at the point in my life where I was able to write this book. Congratulations on completing your first triathlon. I love you very much.

Also to my family for their ongoing support: my mum and dad for giving me life and love; my brother and sister and their spouses for generally being fabulous; my beautiful nieces and nephew, Mollie, Jessie, Ollie and Willa, whose playfulness and enthusiasm inspires their aunty every single day.

There are also a few people, though not explicitly involved in the creation of this book, to whom I will forever be grateful. To Zoe Williams, for all the advice and laughter, and helping me navigate the bumpy road to making a living as a freelance writer. To Rebecca de Pelet, Lucy Pollock and James Methven for encouraging my literary endeavours all those years ago. To Emmy Gilmour, David Gilmour and Ann Davis, without whose compassion, kindness and expertise I doubt I'd ever have come this far.

Most importantly, huge thanks goes to those who helped *Run, Ride, Sink or Swim* come to fruition. To my ever faithful agent and lovely friend, Kate McLennan, and the team at Abner Stein: thank you for always believing in me, especially when I was struggling with ideas, feeling hopeless and unsure what came next . . . I'm sure I'm not the first (and won't be the last) author whom you've kept sane with your diplomacy and good humour. To my fantastic editor, Sarah Savitt, and all at Faber – your sensitivity and hard work was limitless; I feel very blessed to have you on my side and have truly loved getting to know you as well as the process of working together.

To Rob Popper and Salim Ahmed, for quality coaching, excellent coffee and thought-provoking conversation. To triathletes Ren, Emily, Suzanne, Paula, Jodie, Hollie and Olivia – thank you for giving me an insight into your world and being so generous with your time. To paratriathlete Jane Egan – thank you for all the information, advice and for trusting me with your story. You remain a great source of inspiration and I feel privileged to have spent that rainy day together in Glasgow. To Emily Chappell: thank you for your ebullient support in Newcastle and, of course, for fixing that tyre. To Barry and Gus: your unwavering efforts to keep my body from breaking was/is appreciated. To the Property Manager, Raymond, in St Lucia for lending me your daughter's bike less than ninety seconds after meeting me. To our long-haired ginger tomcat, Jeffrey, for moulting all over the pages that had to go. And, of course, to the entire triathlon community for welcoming me into your exhilarating, addictive world, and teaching me that *I can handle it.*